The Book of Boaz

Or

It's amazing what you can do when you don't know what you can't do!

Dave Smith

First published in Great Britain in 2014

Instant Apostle
The Barn
1 Watford House Lane
Watford
Herts
WD17 1BJ

British Library Cataloguing-in-Publication Data

A catalogue record for this book is available from the British Library

This book and all other Instant Apostle books are available from Instant Apostle:

Website: www.instantapostle.com

E-mail: info@instantapostle.com

ISBN 978-1-909728-17-2

Printed in Great Britain

Instant Apostle is a new way of getting ideas flowing, between followers of Jesus, and between those who would like to know more about His Kingdom.

It's not just about books and it's not about a one-way information flow. It's about building a community where ideas are exchanged. Ideas will be expressed at an appropriate length. Some will take the form of books. But in many cases ideas can be expressed more briefly than in a book. Short books, or pamphlets, will be an important part of what we provide. As with pamphlets of old, these are likely to be opinionated, and produced quickly so that the community can discuss them.

Well-known authors are welcome, but we also welcome new writers. We are looking for prophetic voices, authentic and original ideas, produced at any length; quick and relevant, insightful and opinionated. And as the name implies, these will be released very quickly, either as Kindle books or printed texts or both.

Join the community. Get reading, get writing and get discussing!

Contents

Acknowledgements

To those who reviewed the book, for your honesty and encouragement – my wife Shona, sister Sue, daughter Jess, Beth, Hillary, Mike A and especially Mike K for your corrections of my inaccuracies!

And to those who have waited so long and so patiently for freedom and safety, and have taught me so much about patience and endurance in the face of unjust suffering. May you all have peace, joy and a future in which you can fulfil your destiny without fear.

Cover picture by Beth Howe (www.bethanyfaith.co.uk) and used with her permission, and photograph by Dean Brocklehurst of Rubber Goat Films (www.rubbergoatfilms.com).

Foreword

I once read an article called 'The unreasonable person'. It made a point that stuck with me. I had expected the article to focus on how frustrating unreasonable people can be, but its thrust was rather different: we need unreasonable people to help society change. They are the only ones who will stick their necks out to challenge the status quo and help the rest of us to see beyond it to a better future. They also help us to extend ourselves personally as we catch the vision and play a part in bringing it into existence.

In the pages of this book you will read the story of the Boaz Trust and will gain a comprehensive insight into the experiences of asylum seekers and refugees in the UK – the good, the bad and the downright ugly. You will also encounter Dave Smith who is, most definitely, an unreasonable person. His particular *domain of unreasonableness* is concerned with helping us all, and the church in particular, to notice and discover God's heart for the marginalised people around us. He has a track record of creating living, breathing organisations that respond with compassion to the needs of the marginalised, and of releasing staff, volunteers and supporters into a vocation of love and service.

Dave has a gift of 'starting things' – of engaging and then assembling people around meeting needs and confronting injustice. Those of us who have become involved look back not quite believing either what has happened or what Dave persuaded us to do... but we look back with a smile, and with our own life-affirming stories to tell.

Please strap yourself in and prepare to be taken on a journey into the world of UK asylum seekers with Dave as your guide. Expect unreasonable and hard-hitting commentary and phraseology that I personally would have edited out, and be ready to express disbelief, to laugh and to cry as you meet real people and hear their stories.

Mike Arundale, Chair of Trustees

Introduction

In 1992 I began to volunteer on a Sunday soup run in Manchester, England. Since then, encountering the poor and needy first hand has revolutionised my life. Every Sunday night I would come home with my head full of challenging thoughts, vivid impressions of damaged people I had met and plans for changing the world. I could never get to sleep until I had spent at least two hours winding down, and I rarely started the working week after a proper night's rest. After one of those adrenalin-filled evenings I remember thinking, 'This is what I should have been doing all along!' I had belatedly discovered what God was calling me to do with my life.

Over the last 19 years my life has become more and more taken up with those who are marginalised and excluded from society. When I was a teacher (and, as my students will tell you, not a very good one), I often dreamed of retirement, even though it was a long way away. Now I can't imagine retiring. I feel more alive than ever, and younger than I did 20 years ago.

I set up the Mustard Tree[1] charity with my wife Shona in 1993, initially to dispense food and clothing to the homeless on Sunday nights in Chinatown, Manchester. There were six volunteers, including ourselves, all from the same church. That's pretty much how it stayed until 1998, except that we had begun to fill the church garage with second-hand furniture for people moving into empty flats, and had convinced those we had come to know on the streets that we were there for the long haul.

At that point I began to realise that we would never really change much until someone went full-time. The trustees were somewhat sceptical and wondered how my family would cope financially, given that Mustard Tree had a total monthly income of £60, which just covered the soup run expenses. They said they would agree only if we had 20 volunteers by the end of September. By then I had already left

---

[1] www.mustardtree.co.uk (accessed 18th February 2014).

my teaching job and taken a small redundancy package. I began to recruit volunteers, and on the last day of September the twentieth volunteer signed up.

I found some space in an old mill in Manchester; we rented out two rooms and part of the basement, and opened up a resource centre for the homeless and disadvantaged. To say that I didn't know what I was doing would be an understatement. Trustees, volunteers and the unfortunate staff who were supposed to be supervised by me can all verify that! I had neither business training nor a gift for management, and I had never written a policy or procedure in my life. But I knew I had heard from God, and despite my worst efforts and a stack of problems, the Mustard Tree grew and flourished. People were helped. Some had their lives changed.

During my time at Mustard Tree I made many mistakes. Some were due to a lack of knowledge and management skills. Most were because I am an incorrigible dreamer and needed to learn that people – including the staff, trustees and volunteers – are all wired differently. If they were to support the vision, I would have to communicate it clearly. My mistakes could have seriously damaged the charity, but God is amazingly good and gracious. It was going to take more than my blundering to bring down a charity that was God's idea. Now, under new management, Mustard Tree has become far more effective and respected than it ever could have been if I had stayed there.

I learned a wealth of lessons on how (not) to run a Christian charity in my 12 years at Mustard Tree. When, in 2004 I moved on to set up the Boaz Trust,[2] I had the opportunity to make sure I didn't make the same mistakes again. I have undoubtedly invented some new ways of doing things wrong, but the charity is strong enough to cope with those.

I can't remember who it was who first said to me, 'You should write a book.' That must have been at least seven years ago. Since then two or three others have suggested the same thing. I have always thought, 'Yes, one day, but not yet – not until I can look back on a completed job.' Then, a few months ago, someone said it again: 'You should write a book.' This time I heard it differently. It was as if God was somehow

---

[2] www.boaztrust.org.uk (accessed 18th February 2014).

behind the voice. It didn't go in one ear and out the other but lodged in my mind. I think the time is now right. There are some things that I think people need to hear *now*. It will be too late when I am dead.

Who is this book for? Hopefully, for everyone. I am a Christian, and much of what I write will resonate with those who follow Christ, but I hope it will equally encourage those of other faiths or of no faith at all (if that is actually possible… but that's for another book!). There are universal principles that apply to everyone, that apply whether your organisation calls itself Christian or not: there are many who do great charity work who do not profess to be Christian. But for me, I just know that I would have given up long ago, or screwed up beyond redemption, were it not for the guidance and encouragement of the Bible, God's Holy Spirit and fellow believers in Jesus.

I would like to think of myself as a *radical* Christian, though I have my doubts. I hope this book will encourage everyone who belongs to Christ to be just that – *radical*. One of my favourite book titles (and the content is pretty good too) is *If You Want to Walk on Water, You've Got to Get Out of the Boat*.[3] For 'boat', you can substitute 'pew' or 'Sunday service' or whatever it is that stops you living the way Jesus intended. Christians need to wake up before their sleep becomes terminal. There's a world out there that needs saving – spiritually, physically, morally, emotionally, holistically – so let's go and do it.

I also hope that this book will encourage those running Christian charities to attempt more for God, and not to give up. We live in a time of great opportunity, as well as great challenges. The welfare state is like a ship, creaking and in danger of splitting apart on the rocks of recession and austerity. We need new, resilient vessels that are fit for purpose in a twenty-first-century world. God's answer has always been His Church. Scripture declared in the book of Acts that when the Church started in Jerusalem 2000 years ago, 'There were no needy people among them.'[4] That wasn't because they were all middle class – far from it. It was because they were a sharing, caring, giving body of

---

[3] John Ortberg, *If You Want to Walk on Water, You've Got to Get Out of the Boat*, (Zondervan, 2001).
[4] Acts 4:34.

believers living for God and others. We are living in 'Breakdown Britain',[5] and only a vibrant Church can mend and transform it.

Way back in the seventies and eighties, after the 'Jesus Revolution' hit the western world, Christian bookshops were awash with colourful posters depicting Bible texts and catchy slogans. My all-time favourite, which I put on the wall at home, depicted a dog sitting next to a cat on a narrow branch, high up in a tree. The caption below went something like, 'It's amazing what you can do when you don't know what you *can't* do.' Churches are often so middle-of-the-road that many Christians have been indoctrinated into expecting nothing to happen, nothing to change. It's no wonder there are so few miracles in evidence today. It's time to trust Jesus and start walking on water.

---

[5] Centre for Social Justice, 'Breakdown Britain' report, December 2006.

Prequel: A few essential definitions

A couple of years ago I was doing a Boaz Roadshow in one of our supporting churches. The typical format would include some myth busting, a story or two, a biblical basis for helping asylum seekers and a PowerPoint of our work at Boaz. On this occasion, after about an hour and a half, we finished with a Question-&-Answer session. The first question, asked by a rather timid middle-aged lady, has transformed every presentation I have given since, and is the reason for this prequel.

'Excuse me,' she said, 'I'm not quite clear... what exactly *is* an asylum seeker?'

I had committed the most basic and cardinal of all sins, which had rendered the brilliant (in my humble opinion) previous hour and a half a fairly meaningless exercise for many of the congregation. *I hadn't actually explained what an asylum seeker was.*

So, right at the beginning of this book, I will start by assuming that, like the vast majority of the British population, you have not been inducted into the definitions and categories within the asylum system. Hopefully my attempts at explaining the differences will help not hinder. The basics are thus:

Asylum seeker: An asylum seeker is 'someone who has lodged an application for protection on the basis of the 1954 Refugee Convention or Article 3 of the European Court of Human Rights (ECHR)'.[6]

The UK has, like most countries in the world (currently 148), signed up to the Refugee Convention, so asylum seekers have a right to claim

---

[6] Definition from the 1954 Refugee Convention. The Convention was framed in 1951 and became law in 1954. For a good overview and explanation of why it was introduced, check out the entry in Wikipedia:
http://en.wikipedia.org/wiki/Convention_relating_to_the_Status_of_Refugees
(accessed 7th March 2014). Article 3 states that 'no one shall be subjected to torture or to inhuman or degrading treatment or punishment'. European Convention on Human Rights: Convention for the Protection of Human Rights and Fundamental Freedoms, Rome, 4th November 1950.

asylum here. **Asylum seekers are those who are still awaiting a final decision on their claim** (hence the term 'asylum *seeker*'). If someone has claimed asylum, they are *not* an illegal immigrant.

Refugee: A refugee is a person who, 'owing to a well-founded fear of being persecuted for reasons of race, religion, nationality, membership of a particular social group, or political opinion, is outside the country of his nationality, and is unable to or, owing to such fear, is unwilling to avail himself of the protection of that country...'[7] In other words, it refers to **someone who has claimed asylum and their claim has been accepted. This means they have the right to stay in the country**. Unfortunately there now are a number of types of 'Leave to Remain', from two and a half years to indefinite – and UK governments are constantly changing them.

Failed asylum seeker: This is a horrible term – 'refused' is a much nicer, and more accurate, adjective. It applies to **someone whose claim has been turned down**. At this point they are likely to become homeless and destitute.[8] Failed asylum seekers cannot be called *illegal immigrants* unless they abscond or refuse to report at a reporting centre when required to do so.

Economic migrant: Someone who has come to the UK to work. Most are from EU countries such as Poland or the Czech Republic, so they have the right to work here. Those from outside the EU have to obtain a work visa.

Illegal immigrant: Someone who has not claimed asylum and does not have a valid visa to be in the country. Some have come on false papers; others have overstayed their visas.

---

[7] Refugee Convention.
[8] Certain categories of refused asylum seekers can qualify for so-called 'Hard Case' or Section 4 support, which is barely preferable to destitution. More details on this in chapter 21.

For those who would like more detailed information, I recommend the Refugee Council website.[9]

This book isn't about economic migrants or illegal immigrants. It's about refugees, asylum seekers and – especially – refused asylum seekers. I have included some of their stories in the book because stories of real people are powerful and are worth a thousand theories. Where possible I have obtained their permission, but some people have proved impossible to track down, despite numerous phone calls and emails. In that case I have changed their names and some other details (and put an asterisk beside their 'new' name) so that it will not be easy to identify them: hopefully it hasn't changed the truth behind the story. We have to be very careful, even in the UK, as many foreign governments employ people to spy on political opponents here. Spies are found at political demonstrations in London – they are usually on the fringes surreptitiously taking photographs.

Above all, I hope that my memory is correct. If you are one of those I am writing about and I have told your story incorrectly, I ask your forgiveness.

---

[9] www.refugeecouncil.org.uk/practice/basics (accessed 18th February 2014).

Chapter 1
Meeting Malik*: a whole new world

One afternoon in December 1999, I was in the office at the Mustard Tree charity – a resource centre for the homeless and disadvantaged of Manchester – when the doorbell rang. I opened the door, and standing before me was a small man of Middle Eastern appearance. He was probably about 5' 3" in old money (or 1.6m, if you have no idea what an inch is), smart and very upright – clearly someone who was not used to being on the receiving end of charity, and quite unlike our normal clients. He began, in broken English, to explain that he was an asylum seeker, and that he needed help.

During the previous eight years, since my wife Shona and I had founded the charity, we had come across a whole variety of people who had needed help. Many had drug and alcohol dependencies. Others had mental health problems. Some were isolated, lonely, and finding it difficult to cope with life. Some had simply fallen on hard times, perhaps due to a relationship breakdown. Every one was unique and had their own story to tell, but I could see immediately that this man was different from anyone else I had met. Sure, I knew what asylum seekers were, having come across some of the issues earlier in my life when I was a German teacher (the Germans have been dealing with asylum issues since the sixties, long before they affected us in the UK), but I had never actually met a real live asylum seeker. Little did I know that this encounter was going to change my life forever.

When he showed me his asylum documents, I saw that they stated his first name as Malik, so that's what I called him. It was only much later I learned that the Home Office had got his names in the wrong order and that his given name was Yusuf*. Malik was his father's name. It was the first Home Office error I had seen. Unfortunately it would not be the last, and certainly not the worst.

Bit by bit I learned that Malik had come to the UK to seek asylum, and whilst waiting for a decision had been given a one-bedroomed flat on the fourteenth floor of a block of flats in Hulme, not far from

Manchester city centre. At that time asylum seekers were not given cash benefits: they were given vouchers, worth 70% of income support – and in Manchester there were only three places where they could be redeemed. The nearest was two miles away at a continental store. Without cash there was no way he could take a bus, so every week Malik set off on foot to do his shopping, returning on foot with a selection of groceries and household items.

I remember visiting the store once, after exchanging one of Malik's vouchers for cash – just to enable him to catch an occasional bus or top up his phone. It struck me that the selection of items was incredibly limiting: there were few electrical items, no clothing, and no pharmacy. When I went to his flat, I was appalled to see that it was virtually empty. He had been given a bed and a cooker by the Manchester Asylum Team. There were no carpets on the floor, no curtains at the windows, no pans in the kitchen, and no kettle. No wonder he was after anything we could provide at the Mustard Tree! Over the next few weeks we found him an old computer so he could study: he was desperate to practise medicine, but without good English and experience of the British medical system, that was impossible. He came to the centre two or three times a week, and soon the flat had carpets, curtains and enough furniture to be able to call it home.

Malik was the first of many asylum seekers who came to the Mustard Tree, because it was pretty much the only place in Manchester where you could get things for free. Within a few weeks the news had begun to spread, and the monoculture became a multiculture as penniless Afghans, Zimbabweans, Rwandans, Angolans and Czech Roma followed him through the charity's front door. My learning curve had well and truly begun, but the meeting with Malik remains etched in my memory, as does his story, which I share below.

I am pleased to say that Malik was eventually granted refugee status, and later his wife and son joined him in the UK. In 2008 he was accepted as a member of the BMA, and he is now working in the medical profession somewhere in the UK.

Malik's story

Malik was an eye surgeon in the Iraqi Army at the time of Saddam Hussein's dictatorship. By Middle Eastern standards he was relatively wealthy, with a large house that he shared with his wife and young son, and two cars. Life was okay, until the day he was asked to go to one of Saddam's death camps, where political opponents and other undesirables were held, tortured and often killed. He was told to go and sign the death certificates – falsifying, of course, the cause of death. At first he refused – after all, he was an eye surgeon, not a coroner. However, a visit late one night from the local policeman and what he assumed was a member of the Iraqi Secret Service persuaded him that it might be in his best interest to do as he was told. So he went – but though he signed the certificates, he did not state the cause of death. That act of disobedience was enough to get him arrested and he was himself held on death row in the very same camp.

At this point Malik's story may begin to seem a little fanciful, but there are two reasons why I totally believe it. One is that I have heard countless similar stories from Asia, and especially Africa, where judicial systems are vastly different from those in Western Europe: jails are not always secure, and poorly paid guards are frequently open to bribes. More importantly, if you were going to make up a story in order to be granted refugee status, you definitely would *not* have come up with this one!

After some time in jail, there came a day when Malik's jailer fell asleep – with the door unlocked. Malik crept out in his stockinged feet, climbed the interior wall, made it to the perimeter fence and found a hole big enough to crawl through. He flagged down a passing bus and managed to get home. Whilst he was in jail, his wife had been busy selling his cars and raising enough money (the going rate at the time was US$ 5,000) to hire a guide and purchase a false passport. The guide took him through the Kurdish area of Northern Iraq and put him in the back of a lorry when they had crossed the Turkish border. From there he was transported, along with several other men, into Western Europe, on a false Greek passport. Their instructions were simple: keep quiet, don't ask questions, and keep out of sight. Every so often the lorry would stop by a field in the country where they were let out to go to the toilet and stretch their legs, and then it was back in the lorry for the next stage of the journey. Most of the time they had no idea which country they were in; they knew only that they were going to a place where they would be safe.[10]

Eventually the lorry stopped in Paris. Malik was told he was going to the UK and was given a ticket for the Eurostar. When he reached the station, he was walking up to the train when he was stopped by a guard, who asked Malik for his passport. The guard took one look at it and said, 'You're not Greek – say something to me in Greek.'

Thankfully Malik's French was better than his English, and he replied, 'If I say something to you in Greek, will you understand it?'

'No,' the guard replied.

'Well, there you are then,' Malik retorted. Amazingly, the guard let him on the train!

It must be remembered that this took place in 1999, before the scandal of the haphazard refugee camp at Sangatte,[11] the media frenzy over thousands of Afghans trying to board lorries and trains in an attempt to cross the channel, and the subsequent crackdown by border patrols, which has since reduced the number of successful attempts to a tiny trickle. If his escape had taken place a year or two later, Malik would never have been able to board that train to the UK.

---

[10] Those who are brought to the UK by agents rarely know their destination. They just know they are heading to safety in the West. Despite government and media talk of our welfare state being a 'pull factor', no academic study has ever been able to verify this. Indeed, research seems to suggest that the main reasons are the 'push factors' of war and oppression. As Prior and Holman concluded in the report 'Asylum Matters' (Centre for Social Justice, Executive Summary, 2008), p.3:

> Though the causes of the fluctuation in numbers of applicants to the UK over the past 10 years are intertwined and complex, it is clear that they are mainly global. There is a correlation between the highest numbers of applicants and the countries that are war torn or under political oppression … This surely dispels the myth that UK domestic 'pull factors' are the main reasons for people coming to the UK.

[11] Sangatte was a refugee camp near Calais. In 1999 the French requisitioned a former Eurotunnel building to house about 900 asylum seekers. It eventually held nearly 2,000 before being closed in 2002 after protests from the British authorities. Most of the inhabitants were young Afghan or Iraqi men trying to reach the UK to claim asylum. Many attempted to board Eurostar trains. Most were discovered and returned to the camp, but some succeeded in avoiding capture. Others died in the attempt.

Chapter 2
UK asylum: it's British, but is it fair?

Fairness matters to the British. Despite having suddenly become winners at the 2012 Olympics instead of good losers, we still have an innate love of the underdog and a belief that everyone should have an equal chance. We hate fat cats that live off others, be they bankers or dictators. We love the Jamaican bobsleigh team in the film *Cool Runnings*, and non-league giant-killers in the FA Cup (unless, like me, you support a premiership team that loses at home to a team four divisions below them. Ouch!). Shakespeare invented the phrase 'fair play', and the public school system was largely responsible for defining it. Terms such as 'it's not cricket' and 'a level playing field' litter our vocabulary.

The British English online Cambridge Dictionary defines fairness as 'the quality of treating people equally or in a way that is right or reasonable'.[12] Indeed, nowhere else in the world is the word 'reasonable' used as much as it is in Britain. It is used extensively in our legal system when judgments are made.

I have always believed that the British legal system is the best in the world. Perhaps it still is. As a nation we are renowned, if not for our fairness, at least for our *belief* in fairness. While we may no longer be a Christian country, much of our law is based on Christian principles, and within our society there is still a strong sense of what is right and wrong. Nevertheless, although our justice system may deliver fairer outcomes than many systems in a corrupt world full of tin-pot dictators and egomaniacal leaders, I have come to see how far short it falls of the standards of justice set out in the Bible.

By the time I met Malik, I had spent seven years working with the homeless and disadvantaged at the Mustard Tree, and I had already begun to question how fair our society is for those on the margins. It

---

[12] http://dictionary.cambridge.org/dictionary/british/fairness_1?q=fairness (accessed 7th March 2014).

was not uncommon to come across people left without benefits for weeks on end, or refused accommodation because they had 'made themselves intentionally homeless' when they fled their house for fear of violent neighbours or because they had been burgled for the fifth time. Nevertheless, there was always the certainty that these people at least did *have* rights, even if they did not always have proper access to them. Over the following years, as I met more and more asylum seekers, I have come to see that the asylum system is not truly part of the UK justice system but is rather something separate and inferior, as are the rights of the asylum seeker.

You may think that asylum seekers in the UK should not be treated like British nationals. This is particularly likely if you read certain tabloid newspapers which, in my opinion, go out of their way to vilify the asylum seeker, who is an easy target and has no way of challenging their assertions. I hope, as you read on, that you will come to see, as I did, that many genuine refugees have been and still are denied justice by a perverse system administered by people who are, in many cases, seriously lacking in compassion and common humanity.

I knew nothing about the asylum system when I met Malik, but I soon began to hear stories of injustice that I found hard to believe – until I saw some of the asylum documents that they brought into the office. Sometimes it was difficult to understand how an immigration judge could have come to the decision he or she did. One such story is that of Adam*, a young Somali.

Somalia is arguably known to be the most lawless country in the world. Its own government doesn't even control the capital city, Mogadishu: at one point the government was in such physical danger that it was attempting to govern from inside Kenya. Freighters are regularly captured by pirates; westerners are kidnapped; warlords run the country through their militias, extorting bribes on virtually every street corner. Large clans bully and intimidate smaller, weaker clans. Murder is common. Justice is non-existent.

Adam came from one of the smallest family groups of one of the smallest clans, the Asharraf. Asharraf is the plural of the name Sharif – Adam's family name. I know that because Adam showed me the country guidance notes used by the judge at the appeal. The judge, who clearly had not read his own notes, asked Adam, 'What is the name commonly associated with the Asharraf?'

Adam, who had no idea what the judge was talking about, shrugged and said, 'I don't know.' The judge concluded that Adam could not be from the Asharraf clan because he did not know that the name associated with the Asharraf was Sharif. That is the equivalent of asking me what name I associate with the Smiths and expecting the answer 'Smith'! It was the primary reason why Adam was refused asylum. Thankfully, several years later, I received a phone call from Adam to let me know that he had, at last, been granted leave to remain. Nevertheless, this young man's life was put on hold for years because of an incompetent judge. I was soon to learn that stories like this were not uncommon in the asylum system.

Chapter 3
Asylum anarchy – a system in chaos

It does not take long, when dealing with the Home Office, to discover how inept and inefficient it can be. That was even the assessment of my local MP, a true loyalist in the Labour government under Blair and Brown. Between 2000 and 2002, when the number of asylum seekers peaked in the UK[13] (much as a result of the wars in Afghanistan, Angola, Sierra Leone and the Balkans), it was almost impossible to get through on the phone to anyone in what was then called the IND (Immigration and Nationality Department).

One of our clients was a young man called Peter* from the Czech Republic. He was one of many Romany gypsies who had fled persecution in Eastern Europe after the end of communism. He came in to the Mustard Tree on a regular basis, for help with food parcels, clothing and other items for himself, his wife and young child.

One day he asked if I could help him obtain the benefits he was entitled to. It turned out that he had received *nothing at all* for several months and had been forced to live off charity and borrow hundreds of pounds from his fellow countrymen. He gave me the number of the Benefits Department in IND, and I rang them. There was no answer, so I rang again a few minutes later. Still no answer. Over a period of two

---

[13] Table based upon Home Office statistics:

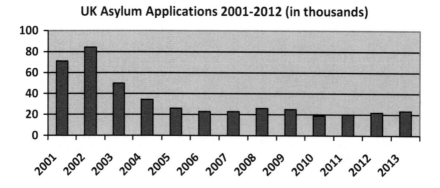

UK Asylum Applications 2001-2012 (in thousands)

days (and yes, it *was* the right number!) I logged 40 calls, none of which were answered.

This is not unusual. Ten years later there have been some improvements in communications. But *only some*. Frequently you are passed from department to department, from office to office, only to end up back where you started. Or you go all the way through an automated system, only to find that it doesn't address the issue you have. How an asylum seeker with anything less than perfect English can be expected to navigate the system is beyond me. By the time they actually get through to a real person, the credit – and probably the battery – on their mobile phone has long since gone. Without charitable organisations like ours, they would have no hope.

A good example of this ineptitude occurred on 14th October 2009, not long before the demise of the Labour government. UKBA, the UK Border Agency (new name, same failings) decided overnight that they would no longer accept fresh asylum claims by post. How do I know it was such a sudden decision? Because one of the UKBA officials in Liverpool told a Boaz staff member that even she only found out the day before it happened! Suddenly fresh claims for asylum would be by appointment only, and had to be taken in person to Liverpool. To make the appointment, you had to ring a particular number. People would come to our office and spend all morning on the office phone constantly trying that number. There would rarely be an answer. Then, usually between 11.00 and 11.30am, they would hear an answer message telling them to ring back at 2.00pm! Then the same thing would happen in the afternoon.

Later we discovered that there was a quota of 40 bookings per session, and after that – tough. So it often took several days to book an appointment. Countless hours of office time were wasted on what felt like an ill-conceived, crackpot idea.

Most of those making a fresh claim were refused asylum seekers with no money, no right to work and no right to benefits. Some were living as far away as Plymouth or Norwich. To travel to Liverpool and back in a day was impossible, so they were compelled to make an overnight stay. Yet UKBA refused to pay a penny, forcing them to borrow off friends or rely on hard-pressed charities to help with fares. And why was it necessary to go in person? According to the then Immigration Minister Phil Woolas, it was to 'avoid fraud'. Mr. Woolas never explained what he meant by that, nor how handing over some documents in person and obtaining a receipt for them was any different from sending them by post and obtaining a receipt by return. In December 2009 Labour MP Clare Short and Liberal Democrat MP Simon Hughes tried hard to get Phil Woolas to address these issues in the House of Commons, but he managed to talk at length without actually answering the questions. The discourse, which can be found in Hansard, the Official Report of proceedings in Parliament, makes for some very enlightening reading.[14]

Could it be that the real reason for the charade, as for much of what passes for a 'fair' asylum system, was to deter people from making a fresh claim? If so, it is the same as admitting 'We don't want you people in our country – even if you do have evidence that you have been persecuted.'

Now I have to say that I have met some very sincere and very nice people working within UKBA. Some are clearly concerned to do what is right, and have been very helpful when approached over clear injustices or systemic failures. Others, though, it seems to me, are 'just doing their job', and appear to make no attempt to think for themselves. And then there are some who would probably like to put every asylum seeker on the next boat home. I suspect certain jobs within the organisation attract different types of character: those who deal with asylum cases may not be like those who carry out dawn raids or those who work in the reporting centres.

As I write, I am greatly encouraged by some of the links that are being formed between local asylum teams and voluntary organisations. I recently had the opportunity to visit the UKBA offices in Liverpool as part of a small team giving a presentation to two groups of UKBA case owners. As a result I have had to rewrite part of this chapter, because my previous perception that case owners would almost certainly be dour, unengaging and unsympathetic proved to be wrong. When I came away, some of my prejudices had changed,

---

[14] www.publications.parliament.uk, 7th December 2009 : Column 125 – Asylum System. Available at
http://www.publications.parliament.uk/pa/cm200910/cmhansrd/cm091207/debtext/912 07-0020.htm (accessed 7th March 2014).

because I had encountered real people – just as those who are prejudiced against asylum seekers often change their minds when they meet them. If we can continue to break down these barriers, there is real hope that, at a local level at least, there will be a better understanding of why people seek asylum here, and why they feel unable to return home.

For a while I have been wondering whether perhaps much of the real blame lies higher up the system, with those who make the policies that UKBA officials have to carry out. One such policy is to grant limited leave to remain instead of indefinite leave. Since a policy change in September 2012, many asylum seekers have been granted two and a half years' discretionary leave. At the end of the two and a half years they have to reapply. They have to do this three times until they reach ten years, at which point the leave will become indefinite.[15]

This policy causes great distress for the asylum seekers, who are left in uncertainty for ten years: they cannot access higher education, where courses are typically for three years or more, and they cannot find a decent job because of their temporary status. It is also a nightmare for the UKBA case owners who have to administer it. At the same time as they are being attacked from on high by politicians for failing to deal with a backlog of cases, these same politicians are doubling their workload and reducing their staff quotas.

Perhaps the vilification of UKBA by our politicians might be seen as a good thing. At least now those within UKBA will be able to empathise with sanctuary seekers who have been similarly vilified for so many years!

It also appears to me that UKBA employees are moved around at a bewildering rate – perhaps to comply with some cost-cutting exercise or a new policy foible. Just when you think you have found someone who knows what they are doing and are able to help in a particular situation, hey presto! – they have been moved to another department and you have to start all over again.

---

[15] For a fuller explanation see the excellent ILPA information sheet on discretionary leave – http://www.ilpa.org.uk/pages/ilpa-information-service-further-information-sheets.html#D%20list (accessed 7th March 2014).

I started this chapter with the story of the 40 unanswered calls in 2002. Recently, more than ten years later, Ros our senior caseworker let out a yelp of delight that startled everyone in the office. She had been on the phone to UKBA, trying to get through to sort out someone's accommodation. She had just managed to get through to someone – on her *155th attempt in 24 hours*, which may well be a world record... although I suspect not.

The bottom line is that if the UKBA was a business, I believe it would have gone bankrupt years ago. If it was a dog, someone would have had it put down, which is pretty much what has now happened. As I finished writing this book the government decided to assign UKBA to the scrap heap! It appears they have no intention of renaming it; rather they are taking away its independent identity and subsuming it into the Home Office. That is very annoying, as I now ought to refer to it as 'the agency formerly known as UKBA'. However, that's far too long to write every time I mention the agency, so I will henceforth defy the Home Office and, for the purposes of this book at least, continue to refer to it as UKBA.

This demise has come about as a result of the publication of the Home Affairs Committee report of 19th March 2013.[16] It details in great length the failings of the UKBA. Whilst not wanting to defend incompetence and systemic failings in any way, I have to note that the committee seemed far more concerned with the failure to meet targets than the failure to deal with people justly. I could not find a single acknowledgement of the distress caused to those seeking asylum in the 40 recommendations. The UKBA has clearly embarrassed the Home Office, so the Home Office has disbanded it as a punishment. Daddy Home Office has sent little UKBA to the naughty corner.

Home Secretary Theresa May has since made an announcement in the House of Commons. She talked of 'a high-volume service that makes high-quality decisions about who comes here, with a culture of customer satisfaction for businessmen and visitors who want to come

---

[16] 'The Work of the UK Border Agency' (July–September 2012). Available at http://www.publications.parliament.uk/pa/cm201213/cmselect/cmhaff/792/792.pdf (accessed 18th February 2014).

here legally.'[17] Is the cat out of the bag? The message appears to be that we just want rich people coming here, so Britain will be better off. Or people who fill our skills shortages so we don't have to train our own.[18] Stuff the rest of the world.

According to the *Guardian*, one senior civil servant told Home Office staff, 'Most of us will still be doing the same job in the same place with the same colleagues for the same boss and with the same mission.'[19] Time will tell, but my suspicion is that nothing will change, except that in the future it will be harder to know who to blame when things go wrong.

---

[17] Oral statement by the Home Secretary to the House of Commons on the future of UK Border Agency on 26 March 2013. Available at https://www.gov.uk/government/speeches/home-secretary-uk-border-agency-oral-statement (accessed 7th March 2014).

[18] Our magnanimous Home Office allows asylum seekers to 'seek permission to work' if they have not had a response to an asylum claim for more than twelve months. It may – and does – take months to receive a response, and even then the answer may not be 'Yes'. Even if it *is* a positive answer, the actual jobs that asylum seekers *can* apply for are so limited that less than 1% would have the necessary qualifications or experience. They include, for example, *skilled classical ballet dancers* and *HPC registered diagnostic radiographers*. And, just in case someone might possibly be qualified, this is the clincher that ensures that virtually no asylum seeker can ever gain employment – any job that they *can do* must first be offered to British Citizens. You can find the full list of jobs that asylum seekers are allowed to apply for on the Home Office website under *Shortage Occupations List*.

[19] *Guardian*, 26th March 2013.

Chapter 4
It's got nowt to do with being nice

He was Congolese, big in a corseted sort of way under his XXL waistcoat, flamboyant and, frankly, a pain in the proverbials. I never did find out anything much about his story because he was always too busy looking for designer clothes and flirting with anyone in a skirt. I have even forgotten his name – probably a subconscious reaction to the memory of the emotions he evoked when he entered the Mustard Tree, twirling his carved walking stick, like God's gift to women, disdainfully browsing through the second-hand clothes and leaving them in a mess for a subservient female to clear up. Maybe he was a village chief back home – I don't know. I just know he annoyed me more than anyone else in the world.

Then there was the old Romany lady who took so much stuff from the clothing store there was no way she could possibly have had that many relatives to give it to. She was almost certainly selling it in the market. She probably would have taken the office desk if it had been lighter. It was largely because of her that we introduced the policy of limiting the number of items people could take – and questioning the sizes, if necessary. The thought of her, a size 20+ pensioner, trying to squeeze into the size ten party dresses she had stuffed into her bag was not a pleasant one. I once saw her at an event in a Manchester park: I expect she was there because there were some freebies. I have to confess that I crossed the road, hoping she would not see *me*. I just hadn't got the stamina to cope with her on my day off. I am not proud of my avoidance tactic, as I know it's often precisely when we are not feeling like facing difficult people, but do so anyway, that God does some amazing things.

When our children were very young and we had strangers sleeping on our sofa bed fairly regularly, Shona told them of the verse in the Bible that says, 'Don't forget to show hospitality to strangers, for some who have done this have entertained angels without realizing it!' (Hebrews 13:2). A particular young African guest had some rather odd habits. One morning at breakfast, seven-year-old Jessie declared,

'Mum, Caleb and I have been talking, and we don't think Solomon* is an angel!'

So what's my point? Well, an asylum seeker is someone who is fleeing persecution. They may be a Pentecostal Christian from Eritrea who had been put in a container in the desert[20] with 20 others for six months just for holding a meeting in their home. They may be a political activist from the MDC in Zimbabwe who stood up for justice against 'Uncle Bob' Mugabe's regime of thugs. Or they may be a child soldier abducted into The Lord's Resistance Army in Northern Uganda and forced to kill and rape on pain of death (we had one of those sleep on our sofa bed for a day or two). Or they may be a womanising Congolese chief from the 'wrong' tribe, or an elderly gypsy lady looking for whatever she can get for free.

It's not about how nice or nasty people are. It's about need. Some are nicer than others. Some are grateful for our help, say so at every opportunity and give something back when they can. Some just disappear and we never hear from them again. Sometimes people have this idea that we should only help 'the deserving poor'. The problem is, how do you define *deserving*? I have no right to make a judgment as to who does and who does not deserve help. None of us is perfect, and if we look closely enough, we can find plenty of reasons for disqualifying everyone – ourselves included. Most, but not all, asylum seekers are nice, but if they have fled persecution, we should be helping them, whether they are nice or not.

When Jesus fed the 5,000 on the hillside (John 6:1-15), He did not discriminate between the deserving and the undeserving, nor between the hungry and the well fed. When He died on the cross, it was not for love of those who loved Him already, but for love of the whole world – even those who were cursing Him as He hung there. That's why He cried out, 'Father, forgive them, for they don't know what they are doing' (Luke 23:34a). Only by giving to *all* who are in need, without

---

[20] Helen Berhane is a well-known Eritrean gospel singer. She was arrested shortly after making a cassette of gospel music in 2004. She spent two years in a metal container in the desert. Helen was released in 2006 and managed to escape the country, but many of her fellow prisoners did not come out alive. Helen has since written a powerful autobiographical account of her ordeal, in *Song of the Nightingale* (Authentic Lifestyle, 2009). She now lives with her daughter in Denmark.

questioning whether they are 'nice' or not, can we follow in His footsteps – and hope that some will respond precisely because they know they *don't* deserve it, just as those who know they are sinners respond to the unconditional love of Jesus.

Chapter 6
Why social action isn't optional

I'm an evangelical Christian. At this point you may be tempted to burn the book, but I beg you to bear with me. I have been a Christian for 40 years, since doing a 180-degree about turn shortly after my twenty-first birthday. Without God's intervention I might well now be dead, deranged or in jail, as I was severely depressed and well on the way to becoming an alcoholic. In those 40 years I have been a member of four Pentecostal churches, a Baptist church and a Newfrontiers church. I have been to dozens of Bible camps and conferences, and heard an estimated 2,500 sermons. Less than a dozen of those have been on the subject of social action (or helping others, if you want the theological term for it). And most of those dozen were preached by me!

Early in my Christian life I was taught that Jesus was coming back soon, and because of that, it was vital to tell people that they needed to be saved so they would spend eternity in heaven rather than in hell. I still believe that salvation is the number one priority,[22] though I perhaps understand it a little differently now. If there is an afterlife, should we not be prepared for it? The biggest fool is surely the person who is not prepared for death, since that's the only certain thing in life (apart from taxes, according to Benjamin Franklin[23]).

Nevertheless, over the years I have come to see that what many evangelicals define as 'the gospel' is actually only a part of it. Jesus demonstrated – by feeding the hungry, having a fund for the poor, and seeking out the outcasts on a regular and purposeful basis – that the good news isn't just to do with saving our souls, but rather making us whole again. That includes the physical, the psychological and the emotional, as well as the spiritual.

---

[22] For an understanding of Jesus' teaching on salvation, read chapter 3 of John's Gospel – preferably all of it, not just verse 16. Jesus didn't really go in for sound bites, unlike our modern politicians, but He's still much more quotable!

[23] Benjamin Franklin, in a letter to Jean-Baptiste Leroy, *1789*.

Church leaders today are selling their congregations short if they don't include doing good deeds to others as an integral part of the gospel message, rather than an added extra. When the Church was born on the day of Pentecost (as recorded in the Bible in Acts chapters 2–4), among the amazing miracles, the dynamic preaching and the explosion of conversions, it says this:

> All the believers were united in heart and mind. And they felt that what they owned was not their own, so they shared everything they had. The apostles testified powerfully to the resurrection of the Lord Jesus, and God's great blessing was upon them all. *There were no needy people among them*, because those who owned land or houses would sell them and bring the money to the apostles to give to those in need.
> *Acts 4:32-35 (italics added)*

No needy people – no wonder the Church grew. The love, compassion and practical help on offer softened the hardest hearts, and God's Spirit was then able to change people spiritually. The same principle applies today. If you want people to change their lives, it's not enough to tell them they need to change, or even how to change. They have to be loved into changing, and often that can only be done through forming a genuine relationship of trust. People trusted Jesus because He backed up His words with action. His followers should do the same. Social action is compulsory for the Christian, not optional.

Back in 2002, when the first destitute asylum seekers were beginning to come into the Mustard Tree, a young man called Maron from the Democratic Republic of Congo came into the office. He was clearly in some pain and very sad. I began to ask him what the problem was. It turned out that he had been refused asylum, his benefits had been stopped, he had run out of money and had not eaten for three days. On top of this he had been burgled and everything had been stolen, including his medication for torture-related issues. I asked him if he was a member of a church. He was, and the church knew about his situation. He felt they seemed more interested in him filling a seat, and hopefully the offering bag, than they did his physical and mental state. Unfortunately that's not the only time I have heard of churches who either don't know or don't seem to care about the destitution in their midst. As the apostle John said, 'If someone has enough money to live well and sees a brother or sister in need but shows no compassion – how can God's love be in that person?' (1 John 3:17). Unfortunately that includes a lot of churchgoers – and even some church leaders – who are too busy 'doing church' to have time to deal with the very real heartaches of the people sitting next to them.

Maron's story

Maron was born in the Democratic Republic of Congo (formerly Zaire) in 1971. His father was the headmaster of the local primary school in the home village of Patrice Lumumba, who led the country to independence from Belgium before being executed during a military coup. Maron was a Lumumba supporter, which was dangerous during the years that followed under the rule of the dictator Mubutu.

If you know anything about the DRC, you will know that it is a country rich in natural resources, and it has been plundered for centuries by those wanting to get rich quick, whether neighbouring countries, multinational companies or corrupt and dictatorial presidents. Life is cheap, and ordinary citizens caught in the crossfire are deemed expendable.

Maron studied medicine at university before going on to teach science. He also worked in pharmacy, a job that took him to Nigeria on business. When Mubutu was overthrown by Laurent Kabila, Maron hoped for a new beginning for the country, and joined the pro-government GAS. His first job was to go and help reform Congolese communities in West African countries. This was not an easy task, as many of the Congolese embassies had pro-Mubutu staff.

When he returned to the DRC capital Kinshasa, Maron was told to start recruiting soldiers for the army, which was fighting rebels and insurgent forces threatening to overrun the country. He witnessed children as young as seven being recruited,[24] and learned that lorries had subsequently been ambushed and the children had been murdered by rebels in Kasangulu on their way to Mbaza Ngungu

---

[24] There are estimated to be 250,000 child soldiers in the world, of which 40% are girls. Check it out at www.warchild.org.uk (accessed 18th February 2014).

training camp. Maron felt, as a Christian and a teacher, that he could no longer support the recruitment policy. This led to his arrest and imprisonment. Worse was to follow, as Kabila was killed a few weeks later. Maron's refusal to recruit was seen as a contributory factor. As a result he was promised a slow death, and was tortured. Thankfully one of Maron's earlier recruits, who had risen through the ranks to become an army captain, learned of his imprisonment and bribed the guards to free him. He also arranged for him to be flown out of the country to safety in the UK.

You would think that, of all those seeking refuge in the UK, a case like Maron's would be cut and dried. What sort of country would refuse asylum to someone whose 'crime' was to refuse to recruit child soldiers? He even had evidence of torture, as a piece of metal was removed from his arm at North Manchester General Hospital in 2002. Unfortunately the judge chose not to believe that Maron could have escaped from prison, and his claim was refused.

Now you need to understand that most African jails are not like Wormwood Scrubs, and certainly not like Alcatraz.[25] They may be little more than heavily guarded houses in the jungle. The guards may carry AK47s, but security systems are rudimentary, and poor or non-existent wages make the guards ripe for accepting a good bribe. In Maron's case he was fortunate to have a senior officer on his side, and a suitable backhander enabled him to make his escape.

Thankfully Maron's destitution is not the end of his story. When he was burgled in 2002 and lost all his medication, food, food vouchers and clothes, the Citizens Advice Bureau gave him a leaflet with the address of the Mustard Tree. That's how he came to us – hungry, distressed, depressed and in some pain. We were able to pray with him and help with food and clothing, and when the first destitution

---

[25] In September 2011 eight gunmen managed to gain entry into Kassapa Prison on the outskirts of Lubumbashi, DRC's second largest city, in a minivan. They released a former militia leader who had been convicted of terrorism and crimes against humanity, along with 967 other prisoners. Apparently they entered 'unnoticed'. Asylum judges would do well to note the level of security in African jails before they disbelieve escape stories.

project with the Red Cross[26] opened in March 2003, Maron was one of the first clients. Keen to help others, he was also one of the first volunteers at the project. It was there that he met Bex, the project coordinator. They fell in love, married, and now have a daughter, Rosie.

All this time Maron was a refused asylum seeker. Fresh submissions were rejected, and he was continually told to return to the DRC. Even when the marriage was accepted as genuine and he won a court appeal in 2006 to be granted leave to remain, the Home Office insisted that this could only happen if Maron returned to the DRC and applied for a spousal visa from there.[27] They seemed oblivious – or unconcerned – that to do so would put him in grave danger, as he was still a wanted man, and the new dictator was Laurent Kabila's son.

Unable to work and support his family, and unable to access education or training or claim benefits, Maron eventually decided that he would have to take the risk. He flew home, knowing that, if the

---

[26] Most people think that the Red Cross only works in poor countries, but it also has refugee services here in the UK. There are many volunteering opportunities at www.redcross.org.uk (accessed 18th February 2014).

[27] The rules governing spouses are becoming ever more brutal. In Maron's case the Home Office rigidly applied the rule, 'If you are applying for leave to remain from inside the UK on the basis of your relationship with a UK national, you must have leave to remain in the UK on a visa that is valid for six months at the time you make your application.' Despite the length of their relationship and having a young child, UKBA was unwilling to relax the rule for any reason, however compelling.

In 2012 there were two major changes, which make it very difficult for refugees to bring over their spouse. Firstly, they have to have a minimum income of £18,600. However educated or gifted they are, new refugees usually have blank CVs for the time they have been in the UK, as they will not have been allowed to work. As a result, most can only find jobs that no one else will take, such as office cleaning and security work. These jobs almost always pay the minimum wage, so how are they supposed to earn that much money?

Secondly, the spouse must now provide evidence that they speak and understand English. Personally I think that everyone who settles in a foreign country *should* learn the language, but it is totally unreasonable to expect them to do it *before entering the country*. In 2012 a Sudanese refugee tried to bring his wife and child over to join him – but she did not speak English. The nearest English centre was 100 miles from her home, so she had to leave the child with the grandmother while she travelled to the centre – all at a cost, of course, which means that there is even less money now to meet the £18,600 threshold.

authorities realised who he was, he may never see his wife and child again. At this point God stepped in. As Maron flew home, he got talking to the stranger sitting next to him, who was also on his way to Kinshasa. It turned out that he was Scottish and a member of the UN–European military operations staff. The Scotsman found it hard to believe that the UK government could have exposed someone like Maron to such danger, given the nature of the weekly reports that he had been sending them.

Maron had paid an agent in the presidential guard to smuggle him into the country from the plane. The plan worked until he was caught outside the airport by soldiers pointing guns at him and shouting that he was from the UK. They told him he was no longer from the DRC and should not have dared to come back. At this point the stranger from the plane reappeared and rescued him. He whisked him away in a three-vehicle escort – two UN and one British Embassy-flagged car in which Maron sat. He also offered Maron his mobile to contact his family in Britain.

A few days later, despite the relevant official at the British Embassy being on holiday and the visa machine breaking down, Maron had his British visa. Now he has British citizenship and can at last lead the sort of life that most of us take for granted. And, like many refugees, he is now putting far more back into British society than he ever took out whilst seeking asylum. Nevertheless, Maron still cannot go back to DRC or endanger his family there by having too much contact with them.

Chapter 7
Caught in the Act

In 2002 the government decided, in its wisdom, to change asylum law. I had to look up the actual name of the Act of Parliament, because there have been so many over the past decade or so. There have been almost as many as there have been immigration ministers (ten between 2000 and 2013, and I bet you can't name more than two!), which is some going. Each one has been more draconian than the last – Acts of Parliament, that is – though many would say it is also true of most of the immigration ministers!

The particular section of the Nationality, Immigration and Asylum Act 2002 that alarmed me, and anyone who worked with asylum seekers, was the notorious Section 55. Briefly, it declared that anyone who 'did not claim asylum as soon as reasonably practicable' would not be given support under the National Asylum Support Service (NASS).[28]

At first sight that looks quite reasonable. After all, why *should* we support people who come into the country then decide to claim asylum later? Wouldn't those who are genuine claim asylum as soon as their feet hit terra firma in the UK? Wouldn't Section 55 just catch out the bogus ones?[29]

---

[28] Nationality, Immigration and Asylum Act 2002, page 37, Section 55 (1) Late Claim for asylum; refusal of support.

[29] In 2004 Ken Livingstone, then Mayor of London, commissioned an impact assessment for London of the withdrawal of support for in-country applicants. It was called Destitution By Design. Based on the results of a survey, it estimated that around 200 asylum seekers were being made destitute every week in London as a result of Section 55. It called for a repeal of the legislation.

Interestingly, despite the increase in destitution, the legislation did nothing to stop people from applying in country, as the figures actually rose the following year to 71%. By 2011 it had reached a staggering 88%. There could be a number of reasons for this. One could be that many who came here on work visas are having their applications for renewal turned down. Those from countries like Zimbabwe and Syria may feel unable to return, leaving them with little option but to seek asylum.

Unfortunately the Labour government of the time didn't bother to consult anyone about this particular change – or at least, no one who would tell them anything they didn't want to hear. If they had consulted, they would have been told by refugee support organisations that *many*, if not *most*, asylum seekers coming into the UK are smuggled here on false passports, and they do not claim asylum at the port of entry.

Within a few months of meeting asylum seekers and listening to their stories, I began to see a familiar pattern emerging. In order to leave their country, they had to obtain a false passport: it was simply too dangerous to be caught with documents giving their real name and age. They also needed a reason for coming to the UK. An agent – often a businessman who regularly made trips to the UK – would, for around US$ 5,000, bring them into the country on the pretext that they were a close relative. It was a nice little sideline for the businessman. The asylum seekers were told to keep quiet as they came through passport control, and told not to claim asylum until they were safely in the country.

Typically, the asylum seeker would be taken to another city, dropped at a bus stop or train station and told to wait there for an hour or two while the agent went somewhere on business – and then would promptly disappear. When it became apparent after several hours that the agent was not coming back, the asylum seeker would have to find out where they should claim asylum. Sometimes that was difficult, especially if they spoke no English. By the time they found their way to the Home Office in Croydon or Liverpool, perhaps via a police station, then Refugee Council or Refugee Action, it would have been many hours or even days since they had entered the country. The agent would still have their false passport, which would later be recycled for the next client, and the asylum seeker would have no proof of when or where they had arrived. The agent, who had never given the client his real name, was long since gone and untraceable. We just *knew* that Section 55 was going to be an unmitigated disaster, and that many genuine people would be made homeless and destitute as a result.

Already by this time I had come across a lady called Amanda Jones-Said from Refugee Services at the British Red Cross, who had often brought in asylum-seeking clients to the Mustard Tree for clothing and

44

other items. She was equally concerned about the impending disaster that Section 55 would bring, and had managed to persuade her boss at the Red Cross to allocate some money for a destitution project, believing that we would soon be inundated with homeless and hungry asylum seekers. In March 2003 we opened the project at the Mustard Tree.[30] It offered a food parcel, a few pounds in cash and some toiletries to asylum seekers who had no support or recourse to public funds. The first week there were 15 clients. Within four months the numbers had rocketed to 85 a week – and the cash we were able to offer had started to go down as resources were stretched.

At that point I began to think that we needed something more than half a day in a homeless charity to deal with asylum destitution. The seeds of a new charity were slowly being sown.

Why do asylum seekers use false passports?

Why is it that so many come here on false passports? Isn't that illegal? Doesn't that prove that they are bogus?

In the UK everyone is entitled to a passport. Our system of government might not be perfect, but we do have a democracy, and no

---

[30] This was the first Red Cross supported *Asylum Destitution Project* in the UK. It was hoped that it would prove a temporary necessity, but, ten years on, there is no sign of an end to destitution, and the British Red Cross is supporting more destitute asylum seekers than ever. To mark the anniversary of the project the Red Cross and Boaz teamed up to produce 'A Decade of Destitution: Time to Change', a report that attempted to map the extent and nature of destitution in Greater Manchester. It can be downloaded from the Red Cross website: http://www.redcross.org.uk/About-us/Advocacy/~/media/BritishRedCross/Documents/What%20we%20do/UK%20service s/Greater%20Manchester%20destitution%20report.pdf (accessed 7th March 2014). As Nick Scott-Flynn, Head of Refugee Support at the *British Red Cross* says in the foreword:

> Unfortunately, what was intended to be a temporary solution to a temporary problem turned out to be the start of a long journey. That journey has seen many agencies work together, in challenging circumstances and with very limited finances, to support some of the most vulnerable people in our community. Ten years since the project started we are in the unenviable position of marking a decade of destitution among asylum seekers in Greater Manchester. Indeed, this month we expect to see the 3,000th destitute person ask us for help.

one is locked up for opposing the government or expressing views that are different from those of the Prime Minister. But what if you lived in a country where there was no democracy, and where standing up for human rights would make you a prime candidate for torture or death (like much of Africa and a hefty chunk of Asia, for example)? Perhaps you are the editor of a newspaper that has exposed the corruption of your president, or you have led a student protest calling for the right to vote or the end to unelected government. Or you may be a Christian pastor in a country where your faith is outlawed, and simply holding meetings is enough to see you incarcerated in an underground prison that few will ever leave.

If that is you, and you have to flee for your life, would you carry with you documents, like a passport, that identify you as an enemy of the state? I don't think so. You would have to pretend to be someone else simply to survive. The shame is that our UK asylum system doesn't seem to understand this – or maybe it's just the people who administer the system who don't understand it: after all, systems are designed and run by people. And it's the people that are the real problem – but more on this in a later chapter.

The UK government does not seem to have read the 1951 Geneva Convention properly, because Article 31 states clearly that asylum seekers should not be penalised for entering a country illegally.[31] Nevertheless, the Home Office often considers this to be a criminal offence, and has regularly detained asylum seekers entering the UK on false papers.[32]

---

[31] Article 31 states:

> The Contracting States shall not impose penalties, on account of their illegal entry or presence, on refugees who, coming directly from a territory where their life or freedom was threatened in the sense of article 1, enter or are present in their territory without authorization, provided they present themselves without delay to the authorities and show good cause for their illegal entry or presence.

[32] The National Coalition of Anti-Deportation Campaigns (which has recently changed its name to Right to Remain but is still widely known as NCADC) has produced a very useful Campaigning Toolkit. It helps to explain the UK Asylum System, and includes a section on Entering the UK and Claiming Asylum, where Article 31 is explored more fully. The toolkit can be found at http://www.ncadc.org.uk/toolkit/ (accessed 7th March 2014).

Chapter 8
Jesus said, 'Gizza bed!'

We live in a world that is obsessed with health and safety, risk assessments, insurance and all sorts of things that, in fact, can actually prevent good things happening. There is no shortage of good ideas for altering the world for the better, but there is a shortage of people willing to take risks.

When we first started taking destitute people in, it was purely in response to a need. We were coming across really vulnerable people who had no supportive community and few friends. Some had already become 'street homeless' and were sleeping outside in the train station, parks, doorways or abandoned buildings We didn't have time to write policies, set up robust procedures, research the extent of the problem, form a committee, raise funds and appoint a coordinator. I'm not against any of those things: they are important, and as time has gone on, and we have found staff and volunteers who are skilled in these areas, we have put policies and procedures in place that have made our projects more effective, accountable and efficient.

But the truth is that many projects never get beyond the drawing board because they wait for all these things to happen before they start. Working with asylum seekers is not a popular cause, largely thanks to media scaremongering and scapegoating. People aren't going to fund you to accommodate refused asylum seekers if they think they shouldn't be here in the first place, so you simply have to get started with whatever you have. In our case that was our sofa bed, a few supporters with a spare room, and the belief that we were doing the right thing. 'The right thing' – there's more about the political hijacking of this phrase in a later chapter!

Was it risky? Well, we often didn't know the people who came to stay with us, so, in theory, yes it was. Three of the early guests I recall were a Nigerian lady who had been released from prison nine months pregnant; a young Zimbabwean who had some mental health issues and always wore a bobble hat, even at mealtimes; and a former child soldier from Uganda who looked like he was built out of granite and could have strangled me with one hand. As it turned out, the lady was a real sweetie, the Zimbabwean a bit odd but pleasantly harmless, and the soldier just grateful for a bed for the night.

Jesus doesn't ask us to do this to make us feel good, but He made it very clear in one of His last sermons on Earth that it's things like giving people a bed for the night that will ultimately determine where we spend eternity. Matthew's gospel chapter 25 verses 31-46 are absolutely unequivocal. How we treat others is how we treat Jesus. 'When you did it to one of the least of these my brothers and sisters, you were doing it to me' (verse 40). Included in the list of things we are to do is to invite strangers into our home. Strangers are people we *don't* know. They may not come recommended or risk assessed. They may have issues, illnesses or annoying habits. Not everyone is nice. Not everyone is grateful. Not everyone does the washing-up (especially men from cultures where that is 'women's work'). But if that's what Jesus is asking us to do, then surely He'll take the responsibility for what happens to us. We don't do it *in order* to feel good, but we probably will. After all, He promises that if we give, it will be given back to us – with interest.

> Give, and you will receive. Your gift will return to you in full – pressed down, shaken together to make room for more, running over, and poured into your lap.
> *Luke 6:38*

You can't outgive God.

NRPF

That stands for *No Recourse to Public Funds*. I first learned the real meaning of these words when I took a phone call on my mobile. I still don't know how they got the number, but people have a way of finding out who might be able to help when they have a big problem. Anyway, the call went something like this:

'Hello. I'm not sure if you can help me here, but I've been given your number. I'm ringing from Styal Women's Prison. We have a lady here who is due to be released tomorrow, and she has nowhere to go. We have tried everywhere, but she can't get into a hostel because she has no recourse to public funds. Oh… and she is also nine months pregnant. I'm really sorry to bother you, but I don't know what to do.'

As soon as she mentioned the words 'nine months pregnant', I knew what I had to do. After a very brief discussion with my wife Shona I set off for the prison, picked up Rosa* and brought her back to our sofa bed. She was there for about a week until she went into labour. By the time she came out of hospital she had been sorted out with a bedsit through the Asylum Support Service.

There's a lot more to Rosa's story. Some we found out while she was with us, and some later. Here's the gist, as I remember it. She was from a Christian family in Northern Nigeria. She met and fell in love with a young man who was a Muslim. They married, incurring the wrath of his family, who wanted to murder them both in what is commonly known as an 'honour killing'. Naturally they fled. They bought false passports – at a price, of course – and headed for Canada and, hopefully, freedom and a new life. Unfortunately, they had the misfortune to have to stop over at Manchester Airport en route to Canada. At that point the airport authorities discovered that their passports were not just false, but also stolen. They were convicted of fraud and sentenced to nine months in prison each – he in Strangeways and she in Styal. They served just four and a half months owing to good behaviour, and since she was already four and a half months pregnant when she went in, she was about to give birth when they released her.

When they were released, we discovered that she and her husband had *separate* asylum claims. The solicitors hadn't had the wit to put them together. Not only that, but the Home Office wanted to deport Milton* straight back to Nigeria – they weren't even going to release him for the birth of the baby! Eventually their claims were linked, and Milton was released to live with his wife and child. They had almost nothing for the baby, so friends of ours from church gave them a stack of lovely clothes and all the paraphernalia like prams and cots that were needed. It was lovely stuff – probably not far short of a grand in value.

A few months later we received a call from Milton. They were in Newcastle-upon-Tyne, where they had been 'dispersed' according to Home Office policy. When they were taken to their new home, they were only allowed to take two bags. The cot, the pram and all the other bulky items had been left behind 'in storage'. I went straight to the accommodation provider, as I had serious doubts as to the integrity of this particular company. They showed me a 'storage facility' next to their accommodation. It had holes in the roof where pigeons came in and out. It was filthy, and full of discarded and 'stored' items. There was no sign of anything belonging to Milton and Rosa. Someone had presumably made a nice profit from the stolen goods.

Now I know people make mistakes. Things go missing, people forget things, and no system is perfect. But my questions are these: What sort of society is it that can even think of throwing a heavily pregnant woman onto the streets, just because she has no recourse to public funds? And why could something not have been sorted during those four and a half months inside?

They could hardly have failed to notice that Rosa was pregnant. And why were they sentenced to nine months in prison anyway? Even if they had personally stolen the passports, it seems excessive for a crime whose motive was escape to safety. How can a family with a small child be prevented from taking the most essential things with them when they are arbitrarily moved 100 miles away? And how can a country that claims to uphold human rights even consider splitting up a family and sending the father back to Nigeria?

'Every Child Matters'[33] is a slogan we often hear, and a very laudable slogan it is. I am sure that no one, whether they are in the Social Services or the government, would disagree with the sentiment. Yet when it comes to the outworking of government policy, keeping asylum-seeking families together is not a priority. When families are refused asylum, some councils refuse to support the family, and instead offer the more expensive and more inhumane option of taking the children into care whilst leaving the parents destitute. Perhaps the slogan needs to be changed to 'Every Child Matters, except for the child of an asylum seeker'.

---

[33] 'Every Child Matters' is a UK government initiative for England and Wales that was launched in 2003 in the wake of the death of Victoria Climbié.

Chapter 9
'Asylum seekers eat our donkeys'

That was the headline in the *Daily Star* on 21st August 2003. It turned out to be a fabrication. The *Star* later admitted its error – but only briefly, on an inside page. Over the years, tabloids have blamed asylum seekers for all sorts of things, from barbecuing the Queen's swans (the *Sun*, 4th July 2003) to the London bombings of July 2007 (*Daily Express*, 26th July 2007). Most of the stories turn out to be rubbish, but even if there is an apology, the damage is long since done. They know they can get away with it because, unlike TV celebrities and sports stars, asylum seekers have neither the money nor the knowledge to sue them for their defamatory errors.

A quick analysis of that *Express* headline shows the damage that words can do. Firstly, it doesn't specify *which* bombers. None of the 7/7 bombers came to the UK as asylum seekers. They were all born here, except one who had come here from Jamaica aged nine months. Two of the 21/7 bombers had come to the UK seeking asylum as children aged 14 and 11, and been radicalised by Islamic extremists whilst here. By adding the words 'all' and 'sponging', the term 'asylum seeker' becomes associated in many minds with a scrounging foreigner, a terrorist and an economic migrant, whose asylum claim must be 'bogus' and who should therefore be kicked out of the country immediately.

The *Daily Mail*, appealing to a more literate audience, is much more subtle. Often it seems to print half-truths rather than downright lies, which, in the long run, are far more insidious. It focuses on what I would call 'negative truths', at the expense of the positive contributions made by asylum seekers and refugees.

The asylum system is expensive – that is true. But it would be a lot less expensive if asylum seekers were allowed to work, if people who have committed no crime were not locked up, and if there were less bungling incompetence in the Home Office. There is also strong evidence to show that many migrants – including refugees –

contribute more to the UK economy than some indigenous British do.[34]

Asylum seekers use our hospitals, schools and other services – true. But the number of asylum seekers is tiny compared to other migrants,[35] and many end up working in the caring professions,[36] putting back far more than they take out of the system. I know of at least ten former Boaz clients who are either working in a care home or studying social care.

By confusing asylum seekers with other types of migrants it is easy to lead Middle England into believing that there are far more people seeking sanctuary here than is actually the case. In August 2011 we ran a short questionnaire at the Greenbelt festival, where most of the punters are more likely to read the *Guardian* than the *Mail*, vote Labour or Liberal Democrat than Conservative, and bank with the Co-op than Barclays. Nevertheless, the majority of those questioned thought the actual number of those claiming asylum in 2010 was ten times higher than the real figure.[37]

---

[34] 'The Heritage and Contributions of Refugees to the UK – a Credit to the Nation' – http://www.refugeeweek.org.uk/Resources/RefugeeWeek2012/Documents%20old%20site/HistoryofContributions.pdf (especially pages 10 & 11) (accessed 7th March 2014).

[35] In 2011 there were 19,804 asylum applications, totalling 25,837 people, including dependants. That compares to 185,000 non-EU members on a work visa, and 237,000 non-EU students – about 5.8% of the total. If you include EU citizens who came to the UK the percentage becomes yet smaller, so why do people single out asylum seekers as being a burden on our services?

[36] On 16th June 2004 the British Medical Association issued a press release highlighting the fact that, although there was a shortage of doctors in the UK, many highly qualified refugee doctors are forced to work in menial jobs. Nearly a thousand refugee doctors were registered on the BMA's database of refugee doctors, but only 57 were reported to be working. The chairman of the BMA's *International Committee*, Dr Edwin Borman, said, 'The skills of medically qualified refugees are badly needed and it's ironic that so many are unable to work.' The main reasons for this were lack of familiarity with the UK system and a lack of funding. It costs £250,000 to train a British medical student to become a doctor, but as little as £10,000 to prepare a refugee doctor to practise.

[37] 'British Future – State of the Nation report 2012 – Hopes and Fears', January 2012. When asked about asylum, those surveyed had a greatly exaggerated view of what percentage of the UK population have been granted asylum. Only 14% gave the right answer – which is less than 1%. Nearly two-thirds (62%) thought it is higher than 5%. Four out of ten people believe that more than 10% of the population, six million

What the *Mail* seems to do is to run stories that are true but negative, largely ignoring the many stories of fabulous asylum seekers who top their school classes, obtain first-class degrees, volunteer for charities and make an amazing difference in their communities. Oh, and represent Team GB at the Olympics, like our greatest ever distance runner, Mo Farah,[38] and GB's best basketball player, Luol Deng.[39]

The truth is that there *are* asylum seekers who are hit-and-run drivers with no insurance. There *are* asylum seekers who have robbed, and even murdered. There may even be some who are making a bomb somewhere. It would just be nice to see a headline in one of these tabloids that reads 'Middle-class *tabloid*-reading White Man mows down toddler on crossing'. Maybe it could then focus in the subtitle on his status as a city banker who went to Eton. After all, we are the nation that invented fairness.

Three exceptions that prove the rule

1. **Most asylum seekers are genuine, but...** Once, before Boaz was formed, and before we had a robust[40] policy on referrals, we

---

people, are refugees. And one in 20 of us believe that more than 50% of people in Britain today have been granted asylum.

[38] Mo Farah, Olympic double gold medallist over 5,000 and 10,000 metres in 2012 and double world champion in 2013, was never strictly speaking an asylum seeker. He came to the UK from Somalia, aged 8, to join his father, who already had refugee status. One of the Olympic TV athletics commentators hilariously exulted in the fact that a *British* runner had *'ended the African dominance'*! The newspapers also seemed oblivious to Mo's previous status. A little-known fact is that Mo has a twin brother, Hassan, who was, as a child, an equally good runner. Hassan was left behind in Somalia with the rest of the family when Mo came to join his father in 1991.

[39] Luol Deng (born 16th April 1985) plays for the Chicago Bulls in the NBA, becoming an NBA All-Star in 2011–12. Born in what is now South Sudan, Deng fled the country with his family as a child, moved to Egypt and then the United Kingdom, and became a British citizen in 2006. He set up the Luol Deng Foundation to empower Africans through education and training, and won the UN Refugee Agency's Humanitarian of the Year Award in 2008.

[40] This is the favourite word of Home Secretaries and Immigration Ministers when they talk about immigration. Just google 'Robust' and 'Immigration' and you'll see what I mean. Even better, google the latest immigration minister, Mark Harper. I don't know what he would do without the word. It is designed to show how tough the government is on evil people trying to enter our sacred territory illegally, and how

accommodated a young man in someone's spare room. When I spoke with him, I discovered that he had been a member of the Tanzanian Judo team at the 2002 Commonwealth Games. It turned out that he had a family back home, that he wasn't at risk of persecution, and that he had claimed asylum because he preferred Manchester to Tanzania. We asked him to leave so that we could put a needier person in his place – someone who really would face persecution if they returned home.

Since then I can honestly say that we have accommodated very few who could return safely to their country of origin. They are all scared of *something*. Sometimes that fear may no longer be totally rational and, with help and patience, they may come to see that the thing they feared is actually no longer what it was. Sometimes their fear has more to do with a personal situation than one of the reasons given in the UN Refugee Convention, such as political or religious persecution. Fleeing from a Jamaican drugs gang or a Pakistani father-in-law bent on 'honour killing' is difficult to prove, and rarely results in leave to remain.

Nevertheless, for the vast majority of those seeking sanctuary in the UK, it would still be dangerous to 'go home' – if 'home' is what it ever was.

2. **Most asylum seekers are honest and law abiding, but**... A few years ago one of our hosts reported a theft which realistically could only have been committed by the mother and daughter who stayed in their house while they were away. They had stolen £3 in pennies from a jar in a kitchen drawer.

It may well be that other things have gone missing from the 350+ placements that have happened during the last eight years of Boaz, but to my knowledge no host has ever reported another theft. When you consider that the guests they have been accommodating have been virtually cashless, I think that's a remarkable statistic. It's a testimony to the honesty of most asylum

---

tough we are on throwing those out who managed to get here in the first place. You have to wonder, though, how anyone ever manages to get in, if immigration policies are as *'robust'* as the Home Office makes out.

seekers, and surely more worthy of a tabloid headline than those quoted above!

3.   **Most asylum seekers aren't given nice things by the state, but...**
A few years ago one of our clients, who had recently married a fellow Ethiopian and had a baby, was able to make a fresh asylum claim. When I helped to move her things to the new house they had been given, I was amazed to find that it was a three-bedroomed semi in a really nice area. The house was probably worth around £200,000 (for Londoners reading this, that really *is* an expensive house in North Manchester!).

For every house like that, there are 50 that could only be described as substandard hovels. I have seen properties where the sofa and carpets are filthy, bare wires hang from the ceiling, the curtains have fallen off, there is no electricity, the bed mattress has an enormous stain in the middle, and the kitchen cupboards are infested with insects. I find it impossible to believe that health and safety inspectors have been anywhere near some of them. If they have, they must have been blind or bribed.

Of course, that doesn't apply to all asylum accommodation. Some is quite good, but one of the biggest problems we at Boaz have had in the past few years is persuading people to leave our accommodation when they are granted asylum support. All of which gives the lie to the ridiculous notion that asylum seekers are given preferential treatment when it comes to housing. If you don't believe me, I am sure I could find a lot of asylum seekers willing to swap their home for yours...

Chapter 10
Birthing Boaz

I can't say that I am the sort of person who hears very easily what God is saying. Or maybe I do hear it, but don't think it's Him speaking. Either way, I know that if the Lord wants me to do something, He usually ends up giving me a hefty shove.

When I moved from teaching to work full-time for the Mustard Tree in 1998, I was given a heavy hint that my teaching days were coming to an end. I was given three choices. I could either:

- apply for a promotion, with more responsibility and more work for the same wages

- work half time for half pay over four days, or

- take redundancy

I chose the redundancy and started looking for a resource centre.

Later, when I was thinking about the need for a charity to support destitute asylum seekers, the chief executive of Mustard Tree called me in and told me that there wasn't enough money to pay my wages. Either I could work part-time, or leave with a month's pay. I won't go into how I felt, having set up the charity and invested ten years of my life in it, but I began to see that this was another one of God's 'nudges'. I declined to take the one month's salary, and left: if the Mustard Tree was short of cash, *I* was not going to be the one to bankrupt it.

Maybe I'm cerebrally challenged – I don't know. It's just that there are some things that others seem to think are essential which, for the life of me, I just don't think are so important. Insurance is one of them. I don't just mean financial insurance, but anything that purports to secure our future. I realise that we need insurance in some circumstances – legally we can't drive without it, and as a charity we have to have liability insurance and house insurance – but people have been so indoctrinated by the insurance culture that half the excitement of life has been sucked out of them.

Being a disciple of Jesus means living a life where the only true security comes from trusting God. When He called the fishermen, they left their livelihoods behind.[41] Matthew left his tax booth.[42] When one man said he wanted to follow Jesus he was told, 'Foxes have dens to live in, and birds have nests, but the Son of Man has no place even to lay his head' (Matthew 8:20). Jesus was inviting him to trust God for accommodation on a daily basis. Jesus had no reserves policy, no savings account. He did not ring ahead and book rooms for 13 – yet they never lacked a place to stay or food to eat for all the three years they travelled the country. God provided. And why wouldn't He? After all, it was His own Son, and His Son's friends, that He was providing for.

In the same way, why would God *not* provide what I needed to start a new project? If it really *was* Him shoving me in that direction, I had no doubt that there would be provision along the way – and I soon discovered that there was. When I went full-time with the Mustard Tree, I had no wages, but I did have enough money from the redundancy to last about four months. This time it would be my wife Shona's part-time wage that we would be living off if God didn't come through – and with two children and a lot of outgoings, that would have been pretty difficult.

People in our church – South Manchester Family Church – knew that I had left my job, and the leaders had been incredibly supportive during the difficult months leading up to the move, but I never asked for help for myself, believing that if I was in God's will, then help would come. I did, however, spend a lot of time telling people about the needs of the destitute, and within a few weeks the elders of the church had offered me a small room within the church from which to work. When they found out that I had no income, the church funded me for three months, until I had accessed other sources. God knows our needs, and He has all the resources to meet them – but it rarely floats down from heaven. More often than not He uses ordinary people with big hearts to meet them.

---

[41] Mark1:16-20.
[42] Matthew 9:9.

From that tiny office I began to put into practice the plan that had been forming in my head for many months, and first on the agenda was the need for a name for the new venture, and a bunch of good trustees.

Chapter 11
What's in a name?

Names always strike me as really important. They say something about what you are doing. I had already spent some time searching the Bible to see whether God had anything to say about asylum seekers. Not surprisingly, given that there were open borders in those days and therefore no need to 'seek asylum', I drew a blank. There was, however, lots of stuff about the way foreigners should be treated, much of which I had never really seen before – or at least, I had never seen the vast amount there was. I discovered that God was always telling the Israelites to remember what it had been like to be enslaved in a foreign land, mistreated by the Egyptians, made to feel like second-class citizens – and forever telling them that they must *never* treat foreigners living with them like that. He even tells them that they should be treated 'like native-born Israelites'.[43]

Then I discovered that it wasn't the British who had invented the welfare state. When the Israelites were given the Promised Land, they were instructed, at harvest time, to leave the edges of the fields for the poor, the widows and the foreigners.[44] They could come and glean, and find enough corn to feed themselves from what was left or missed by the harvesters. There were no *Trespassers will be Prosecuted* signs on the fields. In the same way, landowners were instructed to only harvest their grapes once – anything maturing later was there for the poor, the widows and the foreigners. The great thing about this welfare state was that it wasn't a handout for the lazy – they had to work hard for it – but it was enough to live on provided the landowners took God's orders seriously.

---

[43] Leviticus 19:33-34 says:
> Do not take advantage of foreigners who live among you in your land. Treat them like native-born Israelites, and love them as you love yourself.
> Remember that you were once foreigners living in the land of Egypt. I am the LORD your God.

[44] Leviticus 19:9-10; 23:22.

There is one story in the Bible that combines all that I have just mentioned – the poor, widows, foreigners and the welfare state. It's the story of Ruth. For those unfamiliar with it, Ruth is a lady from Moab, a country that bordered Israel, roughly where Jordan is situated now. When famine comes to Israel, (presumably because they have already stopped obeying God's commands[45]), Elimelech, his wife Naomi and his two sons Mahlon and Kilion, all leave their home town of Bethlehem and head for Moab, where there is no famine. Once there, the two boys marry local girls, one of whom is called Ruth. Eventually all the males die, leaving three impoverished widows. For the two young women there is still the chance of remarriage, but not for Naomi, who is well past childbearing age. In a society where producing children – especially males – is seen as the duty of the wife, Naomi has two options: to beg – and probably die of starvation – or to chance her luck and go home to Bethlehem. She figures it would be better to die back home, and urges her daughters-in-law to stay in Moab and find new husbands. Ruth has other ideas, though. She has come to realise that Naomi's God is the real thing, and refuses to leave her. She insists on going back with Naomi, to a future far more uncertain than if she were to stay.

At this point it's worth mentioning that there was no love lost between the Israelites and the Moabites in those days. Because Moab had refused to allow the Israelites to pass through their land on the way to Canaan, Moabites were not on the Israelites' Passover present list. They weren't just pagans; they were *mean* pagans, and Ruth was taking a big risk going to Israel at all, especially as a vulnerable young woman with no man to protect her.

The story of Ruth is generally seen as a love story and a story of faithful friendship – but it's also a story about being a stranger in a foreign land. Naomi and Ruth arrive in Bethlehem at harvest time, so Ruth goes out to glean in the fields. By chance – or so it seems – she ends up in a field belonging to a man called Boaz. To cut a long story short, Boaz doesn't just grudgingly allow her to pick some corn from

---

[45] Deuteronomy chapter 28 sets out the blessings and curses that would follow, depending on whether the Israelites obeyed God or not. They included bountiful harvests for obedience, and drought and famine if they turned away from God.

the edges, but he goes way beyond the spirit of the law, and by doing so he points towards another redeemer who would appear many hundreds of years later in Israel.[46] He welcomes her and encourages her to join his female harvesters in the shade for lunch; he instructs his men to keep their hands off her, and even to leave her some extra corn to pick up. When she goes home, Naomi is amazed by the amount she has gleaned.

In the end, Boaz marries Ruth, and they have a son called Obed, the grandfather of Israel's greatest king, David, and an ancestor of Jesus.[47] It's a great story, and I felt that Boaz's name would do very nicely for our fledgling organisation – the Boaz Trust. After all, he was a man who knew how to treat a vulnerable foreigner properly.[48]

Jesus the refugee

The Bible tells us that the Son of God became a human being so that He could identify with us.[49] That was of vital importance in God's plan of salvation. Only by becoming fully human, and by going through the difficulties that other humans face, could Jesus truly claim to be the 'Son of Man' – one of us, yet not tainted like us. No one can say they have suffered more than He did. Despised, rejected, abandoned, crucified – yet totally innocent. He understands our trials and tribulations, whatever they may be, and because of that He can help us in and through them.[50] This is a great truth that upholds many who have fled persecution. God knows what it is like to be a refugee, because He once *was* a refugee.

---

[46] Galatians 4:4-7.

[47] Matthew 1 records the genealogy of Jesus, as does Luke 3. Boaz and Ruth are recorded in the genealogy as ancestors of Jesus. As Bethlehem was Joseph's ancestral town, that's where Joseph and Mary had to be registered in the great Roman census – and the rest is history!

[48] The story of Ruth is a wonderful love story, as well as a story of faithfulness, perseverance and redemption. You will find it in the Old Testament, after the book of Judges. There are some customs that are difficult to understand, as it is set in a very different culture and time to ours.

[49] John1:14.

[50] Hebrews 2:14-18.

At Christmas, churches across the world celebrate the birth of Christ, but rarely is a thought given to what happened *after* the birth. Nativities stop at the stable; sermons cease with the Saviour still in the manger, or skip to the cross and resurrection.

Chapter 2 of Matthew's gospel tells us that King Herod found out about a 'newborn king' from the wise men and, like all good megalomaniac dictators, decided to bump off the opposition. The result was a full-scale slaughter of boys under the age of two living in Bethlehem. Thankfully Joseph was warned by an angel in a dream, and he, Mary and Jesus escaped during the night just before the soldiers arrived to carry out their gruesome task. Had they waited an hour or two, there would have been no gospel to write.

This sounds just like many of the asylum stories I have heard. No time to pack; grab what you can, leave what you can't carry – and get out quick. We don't even know if Mary had a donkey to ride on. Maybe Joseph had to buy or even steal one. Jesus was probably about 18 months old – the worst age for setting out on a journey to Egypt across hundreds of miles of desert: too old to be easily carried, but not even old enough to ask, 'Are we there yet?'

Joseph would by then have been fully operational in his carpenter's workshop in Bethlehem. In one day, he lost his hard-earned business. No time to collect overdue payments or complete unfinished furniture. It's a good job the wise men had been so generous with their gold and frankincense: the 'Holy Family' were going to need every bit of it to establish themselves in a foreign land, renting a place to live and starting the business all over again, whilst trying to learn a language they had only heard strangers speak at the Passover festival in Jerusalem.

Matthew goes on to tell us that, even when Herod had died and they returned to Israel, Joseph and Mary were afraid to go back to Bethlehem because Herod's son was now in charge there. Asylum seekers understand well that feeling of fear, even if the UK government does not. When a dictator dies, things rarely change. There's still a Kabila in charge in DR Congo, and a Kim in North Korea. Same name; same game.

Chapter 12
Trusting trustees

The only people who don't make mistakes are dead ones. That's how I can prove that I'm alive. As I said earlier, I really didn't know what I was doing when I started running Mustard Tree. I made lots of mistakes. Thankfully they are in the past, and God forgave me a long time ago, so I will only revisit the ones that taught me a valuable lesson. One of those was when I was looking for trustees for the new charity.

Conventional wisdom says that you should choose charity trustees on the basis of their knowledge, skills and expertise in certain areas. To a degree that's true, but if you have a vision for something radical, there are far more important qualities in trustees than those. These are my top three – relationship, trust and honesty.

You see, when you are running the day-to-day business of a small charity, you can't always wait until the next trustee meeting to make a decision. At times you can check out the trustees by email, or phone someone, but sometimes you just have to make an instant judgement and check it out later. That's when trust is essential.

Looking back on my days at Mustard Tree, I think my dealings with trustees was the area where I made the biggest mistakes of all. Most of our trustees were really good people, with skills, commitment and a heart for the poor and marginalised. Like me, they were mostly evangelical Christians – but they only knew me on a superficial level. And because they didn't know me well, when I wanted to push through the things I felt God had laid on my heart, the trustees didn't have confidence in me. And why should they? I don't blame them – they just didn't know me well enough to trust me fully. As a result trustee meetings were a real struggle at times, and I got a (not entirely unfair) reputation as a bit of a loose cannon.

When it came to the time to choose trustees for Boaz in 2004, I started with people in my own church, some of whom I had known for several years. They were all people I trusted implicitly – and they trusted me. At times I have strained at the leash, wanting to shoot off doing something new, but it's a generous leash, and a very fair one. The old dog does not feel hard done by!

People often talk about accountability. I don't think you can really be accountable unless you first have a relationship. Our trustees are open and honest about how they see things, and sometimes pull me up when I have done something without consultation or have spent money we don't really have. I never feel squashed when they do that, because I know it comes from the desire to do what's best for Boaz and what's right with God. Honesty like that builds you up rather than puts you down.

Gradually, as time has gone on and the charity has grown, some of the original trustees have moved on, as God has called them to something new, or they have felt they have gone as far as they could as a trustee. New people have come on board from other churches, but always people who have already demonstrated their commitment to Boaz, and always on the basis of trust and relationship. No one is invited on to the trust purely on the basis of their ability. As a result I can only recall one occasion in the last nine years when a trustee decision was not unanimous. There is plenty of discussion, and we may start out from very different places, but we always end in consensus.[51] Consequently I no longer dread trustee meetings. They are actually quite good fun, though they can still be pretty long!

---

[51] Did you ever notice that the early Church in the Acts of the Apostles didn't seem to vote on things? There were disputes, but in general things were sorted by consensus. A phrase I love is one that Peter used in Acts 15:28, when the apostles met to make an important decision for the whole Church: 'It seemed good to the Holy Spirit and to us...'

Chapter 13
'I've got a house'

It was June 2004. Boaz was two months old, we had our trustees in place, I was working out of a room in the church that was about 12 x 6 feet (about 3.5 x 1.8 metres), and I was busy telling everyone I knew what we wanted to do. The great advantage of having worked for a charity for 11 years was that I had a long contact list, mostly in the evangelical churches. One of the contact points was the regular leaders' lunches that took place.

So it was that I trundled off to one of the lunches, looking for a chance to tell people about Boaz. As I was on my own and was arriving a bit late, as usual, I peered around the room to see where I should sit. I remember whispering a quick, 'Who should I sit next to?' to the Lord. As I looked around I noticed Kim, a pastor from the Chinese church. I didn't know him very well but I liked what I knew of him, so I went and sat next to him.

Whilst people were eating, I went up to the leader of the meeting and asked if I could share about Boaz. 'I can give you five minutes,' he said.

When it came to my five minutes, I spoke really fast to fit everything in. The last thing I said, almost as a throwaway comment, was, 'And if anyone's got a house to give us, see me afterwards.'

With that, I sat down. As I did so, Kim looked up at me and simply said, 'I've got a house.' It transpired that he had bought a house to accommodate some of the overseas Chinese students in his congregation. Over the years it had, like most student houses, become a bit run down, and needed a facelift. He had not had time to do it, so the house had been empty for six months. Kim gave us the £5,000 he had saved for refurbishments, so we redecorated throughout, replaced some broken furniture and signed a one-year agreement. In September 2004 we placed five destitute and vulnerable Eritrean women there.

Although I am pretty sure that Kim and Josephia will, quite rightly, want their house back at some stage, so far we have had use of it for eight years. In that time dozens of vulnerable women have lived there.

Someday, perhaps someone in the insurance industry will be able to explain to me why they all refused us insurance. Maybe it's as simple as overt racism, or maybe they thought we were harbouring *illegals*. That's why they need to read this book. So if you know anyone in the insurance industry, buy them a copy please. They need it.

Anyway, it was their loss, because we now have 14 houses, and in nine years I think we've only had one incident involving deliberate damage that resulted in an insurance claim. Our very nice and reasonable insurers have been rewarded for taking the *risk* of insuring *failed* asylum seekers. Landlords might like to take note, too – if you want to make sure you receive your rent, and don't have to do loads of repairs, why not consider housing some refugees? They may well look after your house much better than some tenants would.[53]

---

[53] Some of our NACCOM partners would love to work with sympathetic landlords who are willing to reduce rents in exchange for managing the properties. Others are looking for landlords who would offer one room in a house free to a destitute asylum seeker. If you have a house and would like to help, please do get in touch via www.naccom.org.uk (accessed 22nd February 2014).

Chapter 15
Jehovah Jireh[54]

I only know that it means 'the Lord my provider' because of a song we used to sing in church. Anyway, it's true.

I needed a right-hand man, someone who knew a bit about buildings and who could help with the housing management. God sent Nigel, who was working for a demolition firm. First he volunteered one day a week. Then, when funding became available in 2005, we were able to employ him full-time. Without Nigel coming at that time, we would never have grown so quickly.

We also needed more accommodation, because there were ten times more people needing accommodation than we could put up in our one house and the three or four spare rooms we had. So God sent us three people, at intervals of about four months, who had money to invest. This was the start of an amazing trend of provision that is still happening today.

At the same time we found a Christian firm that was buying houses at auction and employing newly arrived Polish builders to renovate them. For £50,000-60,000 we were able to buy a three- or four-bedroomed house. By the end of 2005 we had four houses up and running and were able to accommodate 18 of the most vulnerable among the destitute coming to the Red Cross Destitution Project.

Christian books that condense years into a few chapters can sometimes make God's provision sound simple, and the Christian life seem like a cakewalk. The truth is that every new house presented new challenges. They had to be furnished. There were utilities to sort and bills to pay, household essentials to find for people with no money, and there were depressed, vulnerable human beings to deal with. House owners reading this will understand some of the hassles that are involved when you buy a new house, and that's when *you* are the

---

[54] This is the name given by Abraham to the place where he was going to sacrifice his son Isaac, but God intervened to provide a lamb as an alternative. The name means 'The Lord who provides'. You will find the story in Genesis 22:12-14.

ones who are going to live in it! When you have to put others in it whom you don't know, it can be far more difficult.

I don't know who first said 'To err is human', but whoever it was has proved my humanity many times over. One of our biggest problems has always been who to put in the houses. When you have a waiting list of more than 100 desperate people, there is a temptation to cram as many into a new house as possible. Do you give everyone a single room, or do you put two in a room? Do you turn a living room into a bedroom? Do you put people in who all speak the same language, or who are from the same country?

Whatever you do, it won't be perfect. At first I thought language-specific houses were the right way to go. That seemed to work well in our Amharic- and Tigrinya-speaking houses for women. So we created a house for French-speaking men. That didn't work so well because one of the men was from Guinea whilst the others were from DR Congo. The Guinean man complained that all the other guys in the house excluded him by speaking Lingala, the Congolese French dialect.

So we then tried to put in people from the same country. We created a house for men from Darfur in Sudan. At first it worked like a dream. I thought we had it all figured out, a perfect system we could use every time. Actually the blissful harmony was more a result of pure chance. One of the five men was older, and a former policeman. They respected him, and he kept order in the house. Another had been a chef; he did all the cooking, hence wonderful communal mealtimes. Another had been a farmer, so he did all the gardening. No wonder it worked!!

Then the policeman moved on and someone else took his place. Before long there was a fight during which one of the men was bitten on the arm. It turned out that, although all the men in the house were from Darfur, they were not all from the same tribe. It just so happened that the two who got into a scrap were from tribes that were at war with each other. Oops.

After nine years we have learned a few hard lessons, and we are still learning. Some houses run like clockwork; others are harder to manage. In general, most residents behave well, but there are clashes, which are to be expected when you put people together from different cultures who don't know each other, who often would not have chosen each other to live with, and are stressed to breaking point by separation from family and unfair treatment in the UK.

Six tips when housing destitute asylum seekers

1. Don't overcrowd. It's tempting to cram people into every nook and cranny, especially when so many are street homeless, but the benefits of packing people in are outweighed by the problems it causes. There's usually only one bathroom in a house, and we all know what it's like to stand outside with your legs crossed while someone is beautifying her – or him – self. Neither can you have people cooking different meals on the same stove at the same time. Even sharing a room can prove difficult unless the residents are happy to do so.

2. Don't put in people with serious mental health issues unless you have the resources to look after them properly.[55] They will probably be among the most vulnerable referrals and consequently a high priority, but if you place them with others, the end result may well be deteriorating health for all. Instead, badger the social services and mental health agencies until they take responsibility.[56]

---

[55] Dealing with mental health issues is one of the most difficult areas for the Boaz staff. We have often referred people to hospitals, only for them to be discharged after an assessment. The threshold is so high that very few are admitted for treatment, yet, if we were to house them, they would cause havoc. One recent client, whose behaviour included stuffing painkillers into his mouth, trying to get out of moving cars, and lying down in the main road outside our office, was diagnosed as not having any mental illness. It was, they said, 'a cry for help'. I think that's probably correct, but it's hardly surprising when you are scared stiff of being deported, and fearful for your wife and daughter back in Iran. After several months in a psychiatric unit he was discharged back to destitution.

The good news is that God has been at work. First came a profession of faith in Jesus, and then, against all expectations, he was granted leave to remain. There is a long way to go yet, and there have been some lapses into depression and self-harm, but there has been a definite change for the better, and it has nothing to do with statutory services. There are some things that only God can change.

[56] The threshold for community care is extremely high, and legislation is complex. Recent funding cuts mean that many councils are reluctant to accommodate refused

3. Put people in who you think will get on well. That saves a load of trouble. If the house functions well, residents are more likely to engage in other activities and maintain their health and spirit – and you will spend far less time fire-fighting.

4. Encourage a sense of ownership. People look after things they feel a responsibility for. Every resident should be willing to clean, cut the hedge, put out the bins, etc, just as they would if they owned the house. If you do too much for them, it will only foster a dependency culture.

5. Mix firmness and grace. Try to walk the fine line between rules and flexibility. It's not easy, but it is important. Often it takes time, and some gentle persuasion, before people stop annoying others or breaking the rules. We need wisdom to know when we are being taken for a ride. If you are sure that's the case, eviction is the only real option.

6. Be prepared to be ruthless with the heating! If you don't, your bills will be sky high. Most asylum seekers come from hot climates where they wear few clothes and leave doors and windows open. That is still their default mode, so when they are in the asylum support system, where heating and lighting is paid for, what happens? They bang up the heating as far as it will go, open the windows and run around in shorts and tee-shirts, just like they would at home. And no one tells them how much it is costing, so when they move into their first accommodation as refugees, guess what? The first bill is so high that they can't pay it. It's the same for refused asylum seekers who end up as our residents. We spend more time and energy trying to persuade them to turn the heating down than almost any other single issue.

---

asylum seekers with care needs. It is well worth seeking out a specialist firm of solicitors who will take on cases like these. For more information go to http://www.asaproject.org/wp-content/uploads/2013/03/fs8.pdf (accessed 7th March 2014).

Chapter 16
To grow or not to grow? That is the question

Voluntary organisations almost always start in response to an obvious need that is not being adequately met. The Mustard Tree was a response to homelessness and disadvantage. Boaz came about because we encountered destitution among asylum seekers.

There comes a time when you have to ask the question, 'What is our ultimate objective?' That determines whether you will grow or not. If your objective is limited geographically, that will have implications. If it is confined to a specific client group, that will also impact on growth.

But there is a third factor that probably limits growth more than anything else – our comfort zone. Many voluntary organisations remain small, not because they have achieved their objective or fulfilled their dream, but because those who run them can't see beyond the current financial situation or staffing level.

Our objective at Boaz has always been to end asylum destitution – period. Not to make a dent in it, help alleviate it or rescue a proportion of those affected by it, but to *end it forever*. I am not naïve enough to think we can do that easily or quickly, or that we can do it alone. Nor do I think it can be done by simply obtaining more accommodation. If there are upwards of 100,000 destitute asylum seekers in the UK, that would require some 20,000 houses. At our current rate of progress, even with all our partner organisations and a stagnant asylum population, it would take several hundred years to solve.

It would have been relatively easy to stop at four or five houses. Nigel and I could have managed that with the help of a few volunteers and maybe a part-time office worker. We could have made sure all our clients were well cared for and that the organisation ran smoothly – but doing that would have left hundreds more sleeping rough.

One major issue was our tiny office. Not only was it cramped but it was also freezing cold and miserably dark in the winter – and miles away from our four houses. For clients it was two bus rides away, which meant we spent much of our time out of the office. Nigel had already built up a relationship with the leaders at Harpurhey

Community Church, which was near to our houses in North Manchester, and when they offered us a larger office space at a very cheap rent, we jumped at the chance, and in 2007 we moved.

But there was a bigger issue to deal with: it had become clear that we needed additional staff. Nigel and I were too similar. For a start, we were both blokes, and more than half our clients were women. In addition, neither of us had a managerial bone in our bodies. Going on management courses had not changed that very much. We had added a few policies to our practices, but mainly because we knew we *had to* rather than out of any deep-seated commitment. It still amazes me that there are people who actually *enjoy* doing things like writing policies and procedures.

Anyway, the trustees had the foresight to realise that, without additional help, the charity was going to end up in a total mess (as opposed to being a bit of a mess, as it then was), with a serious lack of organisation and process. So we began our first recruitment process, and the first of what has become an almost annual structural reorganisation.

Chapter 17
Team

I am, by upbringing, a DIY person. Not particularly of the B & Q type, but my mother and father always used the mantra, 'If you want a job doing well, do it yourself.' It was a fairly isolated sort of upbringing, because the family rarely solved problems together – except jigsaw puzzles. The only sort of teamwork that I really took part in was on the sports field.

I don't think it helped my individualistic mindset when, after committing my life to Christ in 1970, I became part of the evangelical/Pentecostal movement of the late twentieth century, where the emphasis was very much on *personal* salvation and *individual* responsibility. Not that those things are wrong – it's just that there is so much more to the Christian life than that.

It has taken me a long time to realise that many different types of personality and many different skills are needed to make up a team. Above all, being part of the Boaz team essentially means having a commitment to the cause that goes beyond just doing a job or earning a wage, beyond even putting in a good day's work. Team players understand the ethos and the aims of the trust, and are self-sacrificial. They don't grumble if they are asked to do something that's not in the job description. They support other staff, and love those they serve,[57] even if they are not always easily lovable. They understand the Spirit of Boaz. They 'get it'.

When we interviewed for the office manager's post in 2007, there were two outstanding candidates. Ros had great experience of the

---

[57] When we started out, we needed a strapline for the charity. We bandied around various ideas and decided on 'Serving destitute asylum seekers'. I suspect that most NGOs would have used 'supporting' rather than 'serving', but I believe that 'serving' is a deeper and more biblical concept altogether than 'supporting'. Jesus Himself said, 'For even the Son of Man came not to be served but to serve others and to give his life as a ransom for many' (Mark 10:45). If Jesus was a servant, how much more should we be? Whenever I look for new staff or volunteers, that would be my first criteria. Above all else, Boaz people should have a servant heart.

Christian voluntary sector, having worked for Tearfund, and a track record of commitment. She had also already offered to volunteer for us – and said she still would even if she weren't offered the job, so that ticked the 'servant heart' box. Rachel, though still very young, had a CV that blew my mind. It wasn't so much the top A Level grades, but rather the fact that she had already spent a gap year volunteering in Africa before going to university, and a year's internship with Christians Against Poverty after university. I was excited at the prospect of interviewing them.

When it came to interview, Ros was excellent, and Rachel was awful. No matter how I rephrased the questions, she wouldn't say anything that would show her skills and abilities. She clearly wasn't comfortable talking about herself, which is quite a contrast to most people in job interviews nowadays, where 'bigging yourself up' is almost a pre-requisite. Nevertheless, I just knew that she was exactly the sort of person we needed – as was Ros! In the end I asked the trustees if we could employ them both. Ros was only able to work three days a week due to childcare issues, so it meant finding finance for 1.6 employees instead of just one. Not for the last time, they took a step of faith, and agreed.

Why am I spending so much time talking about job interviews? Well, because the quality of your staff (and volunteer) team will determine the quality of your work. As I write, Ros is still with us, and has been a wonderful stabilising influence for the last six and a half years. She has been willing to do jobs that aren't really her forte, and I have never once heard her complain. After a time she was made Senior Caseworker, a role that really suited her people skills, and she is now putting those skills and experience to good use since stepping up to become Chief Executive in September 2013.

Rachel gave us two years of unbelievable commitment in a range of roles from support worker to activities coordinator and fundraiser. Most people with her skills would have packed it in and gone to a better-paid job. She has now gone to serve on a project in rural Ghana, working with women and children. I hope they appreciate the treasure they have.

The truth is that without these two, Boaz would not have developed in the way that it has. Now others have joined the staff team and are building on the work that was put in during some very difficult and, frankly, chaotic days back in the community church. Employing the right staff is vital. I know I often don't listen very well to what God's Holy Spirit is whispering to me, but I do know that I did hear His voice during that recruitment process.

There is a well-known story in the first book of Samuel (chapter 16) in the Old Testament, where Samuel the prophet is sent to anoint the next king from among the eight sons of Jesse of Bethlehem. He has no CVs, no references, and no completed application forms to help him choose. All he has is the Spirit of God. When he sees the eldest and strongest, his first thought is, 'Surely this must be the one.' But God has other ideas, and, when he has gone through the whole line of sons and God has said 'no' to them all, he has to ask if perhaps there might be another son somewhere. 'Well, only the youngest, who's looking after the sheep and goats,' was Jesse's reply.

David is called in, God says a resounding, 'Yes, this is the one,' and the rest is history. David becomes Israel's greatest and most-loved king, and Jesus is one of his descendants. Jesse had ruled David out because of his age. Samuel nearly chose the wrong one because he was looking at stature and physique. It's easy to choose the wrong person because we have the wrong criteria. Skills are important, but God looks within to see what our hearts are like before He chooses people for jobs in His kingdom.

Teamwork

Organisations need very different types of people in order to flourish. Too many of the same type spells disaster. If everyone was like me, we would be running all over the country starting new things, and the bills would never be paid. Boaz would collapse in an ignominious heap.

Maybe that's why Jesus chose some very different people to be his disciples. Some were leaders and doers, like Peter. Others were thinkers, like Nathaniel. There were rationalists like Thomas, finance people like Matthew, fiery characters like James and John, and quiet people-gatherers like Andrew. It couldn't have been easy moulding them into a team, but when they were all pulling in the same direction and motivated by the same love – what a team they became! They were accused of being people who had 'turned the world upside down' (Acts 17:6, New King James Version). What a great testimony to their effectiveness: I'd love people to say that of Boaz.

God has wired us all differently, and when we operate in the way he intended, we are at our most productive and fulfilled. When we have a team of people all operating in that way, it can be powerful! Of course, different personalities in a team will inevitably lead to tensions, but it's precisely our different strengths that make for the balance in the team – and as long as we are aware of our own weaknesses, the team will flourish.

So what are the different skills and personalities needed for a perfect team? A lot has been written about this, and I doubt anyone has yet come up with a definitive list. But here are a few ideas. Some I have gleaned from a recent business course I went on, and have been adapted for use within charities and voluntary organisations – including churches.

- **Creators/starters:** These are the people who get things moving at the beginning. They have the vision, without which there would be no charity, church, voluntary organisation. But they are rarely 'finishers', and they often need others to take over the day-to-day running. They are 'Big Picture People' with lots of ideas, many of which need to be toned down by others. They have drive and momentum; they take risks, but can lack focus. More than one or two in an organisation spells disaster!

- **Supporters:** These are vital to the health of an organisation because they have strong interpersonal skills. They are the ones who build relationships and diffuse situations. They are the glue that holds things together, making sure that clients, staff and stakeholders feel valued and consulted. In short, they are the people-people of your team. They are totally committed to ethos and values, but tend to dislike systems. They often prefer compromise to confrontation.

- **Deal makers and connectors:** These are people who know people who can help an organisation develop. They are good communicators and are able to influence others and negotiate good deals. They have the connections that can take a project on to the next level. They don't generally create, but they know how to make use of existing opportunities through patience and good timing.

- **Traders:** These are the sort of people who love the marketplace. They are in their element finding bargains and freebies. They aren't afraid of asking, even if it's cheeky! They work best at point-blank range and don't generally think big picture, but somehow they manage to come up with things that others can't. They are very valuable people in the not-for-profit sector.

- **Processors/managers:** Every organisation needs people who are processors. Project managers are generally extrovert process people who like to see things working properly – and become frustrated if they don't. They like systems and procedures, and have the ability to translate vision into reality. They are the foil to the creator/starter, ensuring that idealism meets with reality. Every creator needs a manager. Without people who have the ability to manage, the vision will perish because chaos will reign. The manager is generally a strong personality and is not afraid of confrontation. This can cause upset in others, which is why every manager needs supporters.

- **Background processors:** There are many types of process people. There are **mechanics**, who like to tinker with systems until they run well. They are rarely leaders but are detail people who love to improve, duplicate or replicate things. Often they are not great communicators, but they make sure that systems run smoothly. There are also **accumulators** – slow, methodical, focused workers who are a safe pair of hands. Accumulators are good people to deal with finance, among other things! They are some of the least visual people, but they often produce more than anyone else in the team. Finally there are **resource managers**. They delight in ensuring that there is enough to go around, whether that is office equipment or food in the food store. Their role is key to the stress levels of staff, volunteers and beneficiaries – as everyone who can't find a stapler in the office will testify!

- **Stars:** Stars have very strong personalities. They may well be on the fringes of the organisation rather than part of it. In fact, that might be for the best, because they are not always easy to work with! Well known, extrovert, persuasive, charismatic – stars enthuse over the creations of others and promote them with great success. Often the force of their personality is enough to draw attention to an issue. They engender support simply because of who they are. For charities, having a star onside is worth its weight in gold. Like many charismatic extroverts, you can't always rely on stars. They can sparkle and shine, but can also burn out.

If you are responsible for a team, whether it's in a business, a charity or a church, it's well worth looking at the types above. Who is missing? What sort of person would help your team to grow and flourish? Our team at Boaz contains most of the above, which makes it strong and well balanced, but we are still one or two people short. Having identified what they are, I can now ask our Heavenly Father to bring them in, as He has all our other wonderful team members.

Chapter 18
Saving starfish

There is a well-known story, which may or may not be factual, but it goes something like this:

> Once upon a time there was a young boy who lived near the sea. One day, as he was walking along the beach, he noticed a starfish lying on the sand. Since the tide was going out, and the starfish would die if it wasn't put back in the water, he picked it up, went down to the water's edge, and threw it in.
>
> Then he noticed that there was another starfish on the beach, so he threw that one in too. In fact, there were lots of starfish marooned on the beach. He set about picking up as many as he could and throwing them back in as quickly as possible.
>
> Whilst he was doing this, a man came past. 'What are you doing?' he asked.
>
> 'Saving starfish,' the boy answered.
>
> 'What's the point of that?' the man scoffed. 'There are so many, it won't make any difference.'
>
> The boy looked at him defiantly, picked up another starfish and threw it into the water. 'Well,' he said, 'it made a difference to *that* one!'

That is where the story usually ends, but I like to develop the theme a little, because the man *does* have a point. No matter how much the boy does and however much he rushes around, most of the starfish will die. Yes, he will have saved some, and every one saved is vital, but he will not really have solved the problem.

It's a picture of most of the voluntary sector in the UK. Rushing around, doing good, saving some – and missing most. There has to be a better way.

What if the boy had gone a step further and challenged the man? 'Well, if *you* help me, we can save twice as many,' he might say. Perhaps there are other people on the beach. Whilst the man, with his long arms, is throwing back more than the boy could, the boy could run and round up some more helpers. Perhaps one of those will have a bucket and spade. Instead of throwing them back singly, now they can be thrown five at a time.

The extension of the story is as long as your imagination allows it to be. It may involve something mechanised, or a human chain stretching out into the deep. It might even involve a follow-up meeting to find out why the starfish were beached in the first place, and how it could be prevented in future. The possibilities are limitless – but all will involve coordination, networking, planning, problem-solving and a lot of determination. No one can do it alone.

One of my favourite Old Testament characters is Elijah. He was a passionate, fiery character, typically prophetic – and, like many prophets, a bit of a loner. The best-known story about him can be found in 1 Kings 18 and 19. When confronting the prophets of Baal on Mount Carmel, it appears that he is single-handedly taking on the entire pagan empire. He doesn't even seem to have anyone to help him build the altar he is constructing or fetch the water he needs.

Not long after the amazing triumph of Mount Carmel, where Elijah's faith is vindicated and his enemies destroyed, he comes down off his adrenaline high and experiences genuine fear. The wicked Queen Jezebel puts out a contract on him, and he flees for his life. It's clear from the conversations he subsequently has with God that he really thinks there is no one else out there who is on his side, and that he might as well pack it all in – life and all. God has to gently let him in on a secret that maybe, if he hadn't been such a one-man band, he would have known: actually, there were another 7,000 in the land who, like him, were on God's side.

Ironically, when Elijah is restored physically and spiritually and back home in Israel, the remainder of his prophetic ministry is taken up with the very things that he wasn't naturally gifted at – sharing his vision with others and training someone to take his place. His protégé Elisha eventually takes Elijah's mantle (literally, which is where the phrase originates), and his prophetic ministry differs from that of Elijah in two very distinct ways. First, he seems to have much more involvement with prophetic schools than Elijah, so that others benefit from his knowledge and wisdom. Secondly, he delegates much of his work to his servant Gehazi.

The result? Elisha accomplished twice as much as Elijah did, and left behind him a legacy, whereas, had it not been for his painful lesson when fleeing the queen's wrath, Elijah would have passed on nothing but some wonderful memories.

Where am I going with all of this? Simply to say that, if you really want to accomplish something lasting, *you cannot afford **not** to network!* I come across so many people who tell me, 'I am so busy with what I'm doing that I can't afford to take time out to go to a meeting or conference, or visit another project.' It may seem that the most important thing is getting on with the work at hand, and I am totally against meetings for meetings' sake – I had my fill of those when I was a teacher! – but the truth is that when you meet others who are involved in similar work, it will spark off ideas that will, in the long run, save you time and money, and improve the quality of what you do.

When I started Boaz in 2004, one of the first things I did was to start looking around to see if anyone else was trying to accommodate refused asylum seekers. I found two other organisations, and a few people who wanted to start something. So I arranged a get-together, then another, paid some visits, and gave our group a name – NACCOM, the No Accommodation Network.[58] I organised a conference in 2005. About 50 people turned up, and some went away enthused enough to start something in their locality.

Nine years later there are 31 accommodation projects across the UK, from Brighton to Glasgow. Some are still very small, and they are all finding it difficult to cope with a lack of funding and resources whilst the problem of destitution seems to keep growing. But a lot of starfish have been rescued. We don't have much to share with each other except experience and ideas, but because we are in this together, it is making a difference. For every new project that starts in a town or city, there is a reduction of destitute people vainly searching in other cities for a place to live, and there is a little less pressure on the projects there. Those who have discovered a new way of working willingly share that with others, whether it's a scheme, a source of funding or a policy.

---

[58] www.naccom.org.uk (accessed 22 February 2014).

Among the many schemes now in operation are night shelter schemes, projects working with housing associations or the National Health Service. Others use amenable landlords, hosting schemes, mixed accommodation where refugee rents cover the cost of housing a destitute person; there are a whole variety of innovative ideas that fit the unique situation in a particular town or city.

One scheme that is being used in various locations involves putting empty Anglican vicarages and Catholic presbyteries back into use. Throughout the UK there is a shortage of trainees for the ministry, both in the Church of England and Roman Catholic Church. Consequently there are large numbers of empty vicarages and presbyteries. Leasing some of the empty properties to NACCOM members at a peppercorn rent would make a significant dent in the destitution of asylum seekers. Recently, thanks to the generosity of the Diocese of Manchester, an empty Church of England vicarage has been leased to Boaz. When fully renovated, it will be home to at least six formerly destitute people. Other properties have been similarly made available in Nottingham, Leeds and other cities. The potential is huge, but it can only be tapped if people develop relationships of trust, and that rarely happens without networking.

If you want a Bible passage to back up the need for networking, you need look no further than the story of the miraculous catch of fish on Lake Galilee. Peter and Andrew were overwhelmed by the amount of fish – so much so that, if they had struggled on their own, the boat would have sunk. Doing the only sensible thing in that situation, they yelled to James and John to come and help. They rowed over, helped with the catch – and not one of the fish was lost.[59] Maybe that's where the word *net*work originated – I don't know. I just know that networking *works!*

---

[59] Luke 5:1-11.

Chapter 19
Still Human, Still Here

Still Human, Still Here – that's the name of a coalition of organisations that is seeking to change the way destitute asylum seekers are treated in the UK. It is remarkable in that it encompasses a very wide range of bodies, from those that you would expect to be involved – such as Refugee Action and Refugee Council – to others that you wouldn't normally associate with asylum seekers, such as Oxfam, the Children's Society and MIND. Even Bristol City Council has joined the coalition. What binds them together is the recognition, first and foremost, that people do not stop being human once their asylum claim has been rejected. They still have the same basic human rights as you and I, so why are they treated far worse than any other group of people in the UK?

The 1998 Human Rights Act, which was enshrined in UK law in 2000, sets out the basic freedoms to which all people should be entitled. Among them are:

- The right to life
- Freedom from torture and inhuman or degrading treatment
- The right to liberty and security
- The right to a fair trial
- No punishment without law
- Respect for private and family life
- Freedom of thought, belief and religion
- Freedom of expression
- Freedom of assembly and association
- The right to marry and start a family
- The right to education
- The right to participate in free elections

Very few people would quibble with those basic rights. UK citizens are free to enjoy them all. If their rights are violated, they can take their case to the courts, and would expect to receive redress for any violation.

Why is it, then, that these human rights, which we see as inalienable, are not accorded to those seeking asylum? In the chapters that follow you will come across further instances of inhuman and degrading treatment, lack of a fair trial, punishment without having committed a crime, lack of respect for family life and disregard for freedom of religion – all happening here in the UK right now, and every day.

Let me give you an example.

Mo's* story

I have a friend who comes from the Sudan. Let's call him Mohamed*. He fled the Sudan because he had been imprisoned and tortured. Once he arrived in the UK, he claimed asylum, but his case was badly handled; in fact, his lawyer didn't even accompany him to court. Inevitably his claim was rejected by the Home Office. They argued that as the Sudanese government had signed a pact with the rebel organisation he belonged to, he could return safely to Sudan. This is the same Sudanese government that is currently bombing and raiding areas of South Sudan, despite having signed a Comprehensive Peace Agreement with them.[60] It is also the same Sudanese government

---

[60] Sudan has been a volatile and divided state for many years. It comprises many different ethnic tribes but is governed by those of Arab ethnicity. There have been two civil wars between the southern, black African states and the Arab-dominated North, from 1955 until 1972, and again from 1983 until 2005. During this second war many southern Sudanese fled, and some sought asylum in the UK. In 2005 a Comprehensive Peace Agreement was signed, and the South became an autonomous region, but hostilities never really stopped. South Sudan became an independent state in 2011 after a referendum that was passed with 98.83% of the vote. Areas along the border, especially those with rich oilfields, are still disputed by both sides. Sudan, which has a large air force, regularly bombs targets in the South, using jets and helicopter gunships. South Sudan, as a newly independent state, has no air force at all and is powerless to stop this. The UNHCR estimates that there are 350,000 internally

materially from their relationship. If either of them were getting married simply in order to stay here, they would have married a European citizen, as doing so entitles the spouse to residence. I use the term 'European' rather than 'British', because, bizarrely, marrying a Brit does *not* confer the same right, since British law trumps European law in this case.[64] It's a funny old world, but not that funny if you're an asylum seeker.

---

[64] 'If a citizen of the European Economic Area (EEA) or Switzerland is living in the UK in accordance with the Immigration (European Economic Area) Regulations 2006, their family members who are not EEA or Swiss citizens also have the right to live here' (UKBA). If, however, you are married to a British citizen, you have no automatic right of abode, and many spouses are being refused because they do not meet the English language requirement or financial requirement (an income in excess of £18,600 for a spouse, or £22,400 for a spouse and child).

Chapter 20
Night shelter

One of the constant problems we have at Boaz is knowing who to accommodate. When you have a waiting list of more than 100 and space for one person, how do you choose? After a while we devised a scoring system, allocating marks out of ten according to health, age, vulnerability and security of current accommodation. In short, if they had a friend's sofa to sleep on, and the friend wasn't going to chuck them out, there was no way they would be given a place in one of our houses. Most of those we accommodate score at least eight due to health problems and very poor accommodation – or no accommodation at all.

By 2008 our hosting programme was running really well, with between 12 and 15 people being hosted at any one time in addition to the five houses we had for the destitute. However, because most of our hosts were more comfortable taking in women than men, we had a real problem finding anywhere for men who were often street homeless.

I had, in my Mustard Tree days, some experience of running night shelters using church halls. We carried out a pilot project over one Christmas, because we knew there were a lot of people from the indigenous population with nowhere to go at night. The council found out and told us we couldn't do it, but we went ahead anyway, as it was Christmas and the courts were not sitting. In the end they could only slap an injunction on us to prevent us doing it again. It may well be that some of those who used the shelter did have somewhere to go at night, but the majority really were homeless. Despite what the statistics tell us, there are far more people sleeping rough throughout the UK than the government and local councils would like us to believe.

I took part in a Rough Sleeper Count one year. The city centre was divided into grids, and teams of volunteers went out late at night to count how many people they found sleeping rough. That sounds very thorough, and I guess it was, up to a point. But when it came down to the fine print, we were not allowed to count anyone unless they were actually bedded down for the night, so we couldn't count the three empty sleeping bags we found in an old pumping station. Nor were we allowed to go into derelict buildings – for health and safety reasons, apparently. I knew of one derelict garage that was used by up to 20 homeless people most nights – but it was off limits. I have no doubt that there were many similar buildings being used by the homeless. When we returned to base at 2.00am and everyone added up their homeless count, it came to a mere seven...

Anyway, that experience of two weeks of night shelters, mostly used by people who had drug and alcohol problems, had persuaded me that running shelters for refused asylum seekers would likely be a doddle by comparison. Over those 14 nights we had not evicted a single person. We found one used needle in the loos, and the only time the police came was to bring someone they had found who was in need of a bed for the night. It wasn't problem free, and it wasn't risk free – but, with God's help, it had worked, and probably saved the police a lot of hassle in the city centre.

With that experience in mind, we planned to run a Boaz night shelter for up to ten men for six months from November through to the end of April. As those using it would have no recourse to public funds, we figured that the council would not want to close it down, since there was nowhere else for the men to go, either in theory or in practice.

Over the past four years we have refined the scheme a little, and we now take 12 men, but it still follows basically the same procedure. At 9.00pm the men are collected from the Friends' Meeting House in central Manchester and taken to the church centre that is operating that night. In previous years they had to wait outside our offices, even in the rain or snow, but the generosity of the Quakers now means they have somewhere warm and hospitable where they can wait for their lift to arrive. At the venue they are given a hot meal, and then bed down for the night on airbeds or self-inflating mattresses. There are two volunteers on duty overnight. In the morning the men are given breakfast and tidy their beds away, and then are taken back into Manchester for 9.00am. There is a different venue each night of the week: seven nights, seven venues.

In many ways it would be nice to have a permanent shelter, but that would throw up some regulatory issues. It would become the permanent residence of those staying there and consequently would be regarded as a 'house in multiple occupation', thus requiring separate rooms, fire doors, escape windows, integrated fire alarms, etc: it would no longer be a night shelter but a hostel, with all its attendant issues. Using seven centres does mean that it becomes very resource heavy: you need transport for 12 every night, several volunteers to cover all the tasks, and 84 sets of beds and bedding! But, by engaging with seven different churches, we have found that many more people have become educated about asylum issues. Last year a total of more than 200 volunteers were involved. At least one church reported that the whole church had been revitalised through engaging with the men. As people step out of their comfort zone, and give sacrificially, God gives back many times over. Those who bless others become blessed.

The other reason why temporary night shelters are good is that they are what I would call 'effective filters'. No one will use a night shelter if they have a viable alternative. It's not fun having to use a different venue every night. Only those who really need it will use it.

In December 2010 our night shelter was full most nights, as it now always is when Christmas is over. The temperatures also hit some all-time lows for the UK. One night in Manchester it dropped to minus 20. That night we opened up an emergency overflow in a local church. Only three people came, but it may well have saved a life or two. One of the men had slept the previous night in a car wash. I hate to think what would have happened to him if he had gone back there the following evening.

One Saturday morning in the winter I woke up early and couldn't get back to sleep. Outside it had snowed, and there was a beautiful layer of powdery snow on the trees. Very idyllic. It was the week that Church Action on Poverty[65] had designated its Week of Action, during

---

[65] Church Action on Poverty is a national ecumenical Christian social justice charity which is committed to tackling poverty in the UK. It works in partnership with churches and with people in poverty themselves to find solutions to poverty locally, nationally and globally. It is at the forefront of poverty reduction in the UK, and well worth supporting. www.church-poverty.org.uk (accessed 24 February 2014).

which it was encouraging people to live off a Red Cross food parcel of 'value' range food for a week. The two thoughts began to merge in my head. I then began to think of a young man, clearly African, whom I had seen slumped on a bench in Piccadilly station as I had run for the 6.00am train one day earlier that week. It all morphed into a poem, which I share with you here.

Living Ghost
It's seven on Saturday morning, and I should be sleeping,
resting after a hard week at work.
But I can't sleep – and I doubt you can either.

I look outside, and see the inch of snow
that fell last night, crisp and beautiful
like a white coat on bush and hedge,
and wonder –
what coat will you wear against the icy wind?

I could – and perhaps I should – go back to bed.
After all,
what can I do for you?
Will my tiredness cure yours?
Will my sad heart mend yours?
If I cry for you, will my crying dry your tears? –
tears for a land so far away,
tears for children who know you only by name,
tears for the burnt shell you used to call home,
tears for the loved ones you know you will
never
see again.
And even, perhaps,
a few tears left for yourself
in your rejected
hopeless
suicidal
circle of despair.

I look outside again.
The snow is not melting.
No one is stirring – are you?
Have you left your bench in Piccadilly station,
where I saw you, slumped, half-sleeping,
plastic bag at your feet
as I rushed for the London train?
Or did you find some place last night,
some palace by comparison,
where no one stopped you lying down?
Maybe a factory floor to share with the pigeons?
Maybe a bench in the takeaway
where you wash the dishes – for a few pence -
unknown to the taxman,
when the regular doesn't appear?
Or maybe even a couch somewhere warm.
Not the sort of couch, long and luxurious,
that adorned your house back then,
when you were the alms-giver,
the benefactor,
the champion of the poor of your people.
But a worn, stained couch,
bearing the marks of many bodies,
dark like yours,
that have tried to sleep there since
my land,
my people and
my elected rulers
deemed you unworthy of a place in our society,
unworthy of the dignity we freely accord to cats and dogs.

This week is the designated 'Week of Action',
when people take on the 'Endurance Challenge',
trying to live on a food parcel for a week.
I think that we, as a family, could have lived on your
meagre handouts
for a week,
because, when it was over,

our fridge would have been full,
not of 'value groceries'
for those we do not value,
but of things we have chosen.
How must it be for you –
surrounded by choice
yet having none?

Your weeks never end.
There is no light, only
an ever darker tunnel.

Or I could have pretended to be like you,
for a week,
knocking on doors each evening,
hoping that someone I know
will open, in compassion, at least for tonight.
But it would all be sham, because
my bed
my wife
my children
and
my warm home
would still be there for me at the end of my
'Week of Action'.

So what shall I do
as I look outside
at the still unmelted snow?

I will write for you,
my Living Ghost,
a poem,
that will try to say, the best it can,
that I hope I understand something,
if not much,
of what you are suffering here,
in my land,

at the hands of those who have so much to share
but will not.

And I will pray.

I will pray
that one day,
in mercy,
the sun will rise on my land
and melt the hard hearts of your captors,
as it will surely melt the snow blanket I see outside.
And that, as it rises,
your heart too will be warmed,
unfrozen,
and set free to feel and know
the rights
and privileges
of one, who, like me,
is also made in the image of God,
and is, no longer,
a Living Ghost.

Chapter 21
Meaningful lives

I once took a Burundian who had been granted Section 4[66] accommodation to a large supermarket to buy some things with the

---

[66] Section 4 support is offered to refused asylum seekers who meet one of the following criteria, taken from the UKBA website:

> You must meet strict requirements in order to qualify for Section 4 support. You must be destitute and satisfy one of the following requirements:
>
> - you are taking all reasonable steps to leave the UK or you are placing yourself in a position where you can do so; or
> - you cannot leave the UK because of a physical impediment to travel or for some other medical reason; or
> - you cannot leave the UK because, in the Secretary of State's opinion, no viable route of return is currently available; or
> - you have applied for a judicial review of your asylum application and have been given permission to proceed with it; or
> - accommodation is necessary to prevent a breach of your rights within the meaning of the Human Rights Act 1998.

Section 4 is the single most hated piece of legislation ever devised by the Home Office for asylum seekers. I have never met anyone who works with asylum seekers who thought it was anything but degrading, insulting and a deliberate policy to force people to go home. Firstly, you have to prove destitution: many are turned down on the grounds that, as they have been able to survive for a while without it, they can't be destitute.

Secondly, you can be moved anywhere in the country, away from your friends, your community, the city you know: there is no choice. You may be given only a day or two's notice, and not even be told where you are going. Then it's take it or leave it. In 2013, the most likely destinations for people living in Manchester were Liverpool and Glasgow.

Thirdly, it is a deliberately cashless system. Your 'azure card' can only be used in one of the four main supermarkets or Boots the Chemist. You can't get on a bus, go to the launderette, go to the corner shop or go to the swimming baths. Not only that, you are only allowed to carry over to the following week £5 of your £35 a week, so you can never save up for anything. If you are ill and unable to go shopping, that's tough. You simply lose what you haven't spent by Monday morning.

Unsurprisingly, many of our clients who qualify for Section 4 support don't want to take it, and some even ask to come back to a Boaz house after they have been vouchers he had been given. After he had stopped several times, open-mouthed, gazing at the aisles in amazement, I asked him what the problem was. The problem was that he had no idea where to start! He had never been in a supermarket before, much less a superstore. The choice frightened the life out of him.

Recently our fabulous staff and volunteers took a group of our women to the Trafford Centre to visit the John Lewis store as part of the Boazlife programme of meaningful activities. It was good of the company to invite us over, but I wondered how our ladies would cope, being surrounded by such wonderful products yet having no money to buy anything. The £8 a week we were giving them for food wasn't going to buy much there!

The amount of choice we have in the UK is obscene. All the major supermarkets have dozens of brands that do essentially the same thing, while some of our clients have come from countries where the choice is limited – not to selecting one out of ten different brands of washing-up liquid, but choosing whether or not to take the only brand available.

How is it possible to have a meaningful life in the UK when you are not allowed to work, you cannot access education and you have no money with which to buy things? Those who are sporty can't afford to join a club, as our Iranian tae kwon do black-belt discovered. Those who have gained a place at college, university or law school can't take it up. Those who have skills that we have a shortage of, such as doctors, teachers and engineers, are not allowed to use them. Sometimes refused asylum seekers are even told by their case owners that they should not be volunteering.[67] It is very easy in those

---

moved. They clearly value security and community above the ability to buy a few items in Tesco or Asda.

[67] Thankfully this should no longer happen. After a campaign by Refugee Action, UKBA issued the following statement in October 2013: 'Asylum seekers are allowed to volunteer providing they are carrying out the voluntary work on behalf of a registered charity, voluntary organisation or a body that raises funds for either.' For more information on the rules around volunteering look up Good Practice Guide 28 at the Edinburgh Volunteer Centre – http://www.volunteeredinburgh.org.uk/organise/GPG_Store/GPG_28_Volunteer_Asyl um_Seekers_and_Refugees (accessed 24th February 2014).

circumstances, and unfortunately very common, for refused asylum seekers to fall into severe depression.

That's why Boaz has begun to develop a 'Meaningful Lives' programme, which we now call Boazlife. It started with some ad hoc activities like making Christmas cards. Then someone offered to teach English once a week. Next there was the offer to start a sewing class. Now the women can participate in a really varied programme of activities, from well-being classes to 'Wednesday walks' which take in some of the free activities in Manchester, such as museums and art galleries. A men's programme is now also under way. When I pop my head into activities like the sewing class, it's wonderful to see smiles on faces that are often etched with pain and worry.

This is not just a stopgap, a time filler. The TV can provide that, but watching TV 24/7 does nothing for the soul or spirit. By offering an opportunity to use skills and to learn new ones, to engage with others on a level playing field, and generally to act as normal human beings, men and women are empowered to make the best use of the limited choices they have. It is amazing to see how those who engage with the programme experience better physical and mental health, greater self-esteem and purpose in life, whilst those who do not tend to sink ever deeper into depression.

Eventually we would like to see a programme that offers training and education, so that, when someone is given leave to remain in the UK, they have a CV that is full of skills and volunteering rather than blank years, which is now often the case.

Jennifer*

I first met Jennifer* way back in 2001. She was a GP from Zimbabwe. She had run a clinic on a white farm, until it was overrun by Robert Mugabe's Zanu-PF thugs. She fled, along with her family, and came to the UK. I never knew all the details, but in addition to her niece and her niece's son, there were about six children, most of whom Jennifer had adopted when their parents died of Aids.

Jennifer was a very dignified, quietly spoken woman who somehow managed to clothe and feed all the children, find schools for them and cope with the varied difficulties of a new land and a failing asylum system, and at the same time work voluntarily in a hospital several miles away.

One day she quietly told me that the boiler in the four-bedroomed house she had been given wasn't working. In fact, it hadn't been working for well over a week and, despite several calls to the landlord, hadn't been fixed. It was late autumn, and cold. With a large family of children who had lived all their lives in a much hotter climate than England, it would have been a nightmare to keep them warm and clean.

I rang the landlord. He explained that the boiler was old and he was finding it difficult to obtain the spare part. I had the impression that he really didn't much care about Jennifer's predicament and would have been very happy to wait a month or two for the spare part. When I told him that she really needed hot water as soon as possible, his comment was, 'She's a very impatient woman!' I'm glad he was at the end of a phone line, because if he had been in the same room I would seriously have been tempted to strangle him!

Not all asylum seekers come with skills or education, but a large number do. One study of refugees has estimated that over 30% are university educated, which is well above the UK average. It takes money and determination to get as far as the UK, and most of those who arrive here have something to offer to this country. At Boaz we have accommodated doctors, teachers, engineers, policemen, IT specialists, businessmen, and many others with useful occupations. Some of these are in professions where we have shortages in the UK, like medicine. At the same time as we are actively recruiting medics from India and Pakistan, we are refusing those who arrive here fleeing persecution. It makes no sense, either economically or morally.

Jennifer was given leave to remain in the UK. I guess she will be practising medicine somewhere now, and benefitting the country by doing so. Sabina*, a Sudanese doctor in one of our houses, was not so fortunate. She came to the UK in 2007, and her asylum claim was rejected. So was her appeal, and subsequent fresh submissions to the Home Office.

In 2012 Sabina's solicitor submitted a fresh asylum claim on her behalf. Shortly after, Sabina applied for Section 4 accommodation on the basis of the fresh claim. She waited… and waited. After a whole year, her solicitor rang UKBA to see what was going on. UKBA said they had no record of the fresh claim, despite the solicitor having evidence that it had been sent. [68]

Eventually Sabina's appeal was dealt with, and, as a result, she was granted leave to remain. Although those six years of interminable waiting were not entirely wasted, nevertheless, there is a serious question to be asked about cases like this. At a time when our National Health Service was creaking at the seams, the UK asylum system ensured that a trained doctor was unable to practise or even maintain her skill level for more than six years. Now she will have to undergo extensive retraining, all at the cost of the British taxpayer. What a waste of time, talent and money!

---

[68] It could well be that Sabina's file was one of 4,500 that were wrongly dumped in an archive of 'lost' asylum cases. This only came to light during an inspection, and was admitted by Rob Whiteman, UKBA Chief Executive, in September 2012. Mistakes that seriously affect people's lives and futures were clearly still being made.

Chapter 22
Catch – Hold – Release

It sounds a bit like something to do with scrums in rugby union, or the way they fire the discs in clay pigeon shooting, but it's actually the name that was given to the process that we apply to Boaz clients. It was devised by Mike Arundale, our Chair of Trustees – who was at the time filling in as Service Manager – out of concern that many of our clients were staying in our properties for so long that we weren't able to take any new clients as the waiting list grew ever longer.

When we obtained our first house we had no idea how long people would stay, because we didn't know what would happen to their asylum claims. Did they have a solicitor? Did they have fresh evidence? If so, would the claim be accepted? How long would it take? Would the Home Office try to deport them? It was unknown territory, so I was reluctant to put a time limit on the length of time anyone could stay.

Our first clients had claimed asylum as early as 2001 and had seen their claims refused by 2003. In 2002 the number of asylum applicants in the UK peaked at 80,000, largely due to wars and conflicts across the globe but particularly in Africa, the Middle East and the Balkans. The system struggled to cope, and despite successive Home Secretaries pledging to deport all the refused asylum seekers, it proved impossible to do so.

The result was an enormous growth in the number of people left in the UK with no recourse to public funds, and a huge backlog of cases in the asylum system. Some of their cases hadn't even been looked at for years, but most had been refused, and they were just left here with nothing. Many of those in our houses were in that situation, which meant that the longer they stayed in our accommodation, the bigger the bottleneck, and the longer the waiting list for accommodation. By 2009 most of our residents had been housed by us for more than three years. The record is more than six years.

Thankfully many of these people have gone on to receive some form of leave to remain in the UK, so I don't for one moment regret taking them, even if it did mean clogging up the system. However, it did raise the issue of whether there was a better way of dealing with our client group, and it led to a new system, which we call Catch – Hold – Release. It is, in short, an attempt to provide a holistic service, at the same time ensuring that everyone is able to move on at some point, so that there is a constant flow of new destitute people coming into Boaz.

Catch: When we receive referrals, they are mostly from people who are pretty desperate. They are literally about to hit the floor – if they haven't already. We catch them, accommodate them, and during their first month with us we look and see what we can do. That may well involve looking at their asylum case, as many no longer have a solicitor. If their case is weak, we may have to limit their stay, but we give them three months to find an alternative, which many are able to do, even if it's only someone's sofa. Most *do* have a reasonable case, but they may not have the evidence they need – or they may simply have had poor legal representation. Thanks to a wonderful donation from some fabulous supporters we have been able to secure the services of a solicitor. Raj is another great addition to our team, and, even more than the rest of us, he could be earning a great deal more elsewhere than he does at Boaz.

That first month is also important in terms of medical provision. Most new residents have no GP; they may require dental treatment, have hospital appointments to attend, or need to have their medical entitlements renewed[69] – things we take for granted. Our male and female support workers are crucial links to external services.

Hold: At the end of the first month the client enters what we call the 'Hold' phase. Now that they are safe, they need to take stock of their situation. What can they do to help themselves? From now on there are reviews with their support worker every three months. As

---

[69] Asylum seekers who are awaiting a decision on their claim are given an HC2 form, which entitles them to primary health care. It is automatically renewed every six months. If they are subsequently refused asylum and the HC2 runs out, they have to fill in an HC1 form and send it off to Newcastle in order to receive their HC2. The HC1 form, like most UK benefit forms, is not designed for anyone who isn't educated at least to A-level standard, much less someone whose first language is not English. Most asylum seekers would be unable to fill it in correctly.

long as they have an active asylum case, or can make their case active by finding fresh evidence, we will not give them an eviction notice – but they must engage with us and be actively seeking to help themselves. We don't want any more Tanzanian judo players! Engaging also includes attempting to make their lives the best they can be in the circumstances – whether that's learning English, volunteering somewhere or taking part in some other activities.

Release: The aim is for some form of release before 12 months are up. The wheels of UKBA grind very slowly, so even having a fresh claim doesn't necessarily mean a decision will be made in a few weeks. Some residents have been waiting more than a year and have had no response from UKBA at all, but others have been able to move on, either when they are given leave to remain, or when they are granted Section 4 support. So far only three Boaz clients have, to our knowledge, ever been deported – one to Afghanistan, one to Pakistan and one to the Ivory Coast – though we have asked others to leave. Some have gone to stay with friends or relatives. No one is returned to the streets unless their behaviour has been so bad that we have to evict them instantly, and that is a very rare occurrence.

Send them all home!

I am sick of reading comments like that, either written by journalists or, more likely, by readers who have joined in the xenophobia. (Read any right-wing tabloid's online comments whenever there is an asylum story and you'll see what I mean.) It makes it sound so easy – as though they are parcels to be sent by post rather than human beings. The truth is, you *can't* send them all home, as successive home secretaries and immigration ministers have discovered – some at the cost of their political careers.

In 2003 David Blunkett, then Home Secretary, announced that he had set a target of removing 30,000 failed asylum seekers each year. A year later, having failed to make any difference to the numbers, he dropped the target.

Undeterred and seeing a good vote winner at the next General Election, Prime Minister Tony Blair promised to remove more failed asylum seekers than there were refusals by the end of 2005. It never happened.

John Reid, the following Home Secretary, famously declared that the asylum system was 'not fit for purpose' in the summer of 2006. He recruited an extra 900 staff into UKBA to clear the backlog of an estimated 285,000 refused asylum seekers in the UK 'within five years'. While his intention at first was to remove most of them, he found that the only way to reduce the numbers was, in fact, to grant most of them some form of leave to remain. Under his watch the number of deportations actually fell. He also missed his target, as the deadline passed in 2011 and there were still tens of thousands of 'legacy cases' left here in destitution[70] – plus, of course, the new backlog of those who had been refused since 2007!

So the question is, 'Why can't you just send them all back?' There are a multitude of reasons, but here are the most common:

1. The country they come from denies them travel documents because they just don't feel like taking any returnees at the moment – a position regularly adopted by Iran, for example.

2. The country of origin doesn't like the people that the UKBA want to return. A good example of this is Ethiopia. In the late nineties war broke out between Ethiopia and its tiny northern neighbour Eritrea. What made it so messy is that there were more than two

---

[70] 'Legacy' cases are 'unresolved cases' where asylum seekers were refused before April 2007 but had not been removed from the country. In 2006 the Home Secretary pledged to deal with all the unresolved cases by the summer of 2011. John Vine, the Independent Chief Inspector of Borders and Immigration, conducted a review of the cases from March to July 2012. His report, published in December 2012, was very critical of the way the case had been handled. He said:

> The programme of legacy work is far from concluded. At the time of inspection, the Agency estimated that up to 37,500 applicants would be located and that their cases will need to be considered. On the evidence it is hard not to reach the conclusion that cases were placed in the archive after only very minimal work in order to fulfil the pledge to conclude this work by the summer of 2011. This has serious consequences for asylum seekers who had already waited many years for the resolution of their case.

It is worth reading the full report, 'An inspection of the UK Border Agency's handling of legacy asylum and migration cases', or at least the summary, for an overall picture of the scale of the UKBA incompetency and the effect on tens of thousands of asylum seekers.

million Eritreans living in Ethiopia at the time, many of whom had married Ethiopians. Many were deported back to Eritrea, along with their children, and some fled to the UK. The children, having been born in Ethiopia, were Ethiopian citizens: it clearly says so in the Ethiopian Constitution. Yet when I accompanied someone in exactly that situation to the Ethiopian Embassy in London, the receptionist told me he would not be given a passport because he had Eritrean parents. I still have the tape from the little recording device that I hid in my pocket. The constitutions of some countries are, frankly, not worth the paper they are written on.

3.   The embassy denies that they are actually from that country. This is easily done if they have no documentary proof, and, since most asylum seekers are afraid of returning home, they are unlikely to bring proof, even if they have it. There have even been cases where returnees have arrived back home and been refused entry at the airport.[71]

4.   There is no embassy or consulate in the UK. I first came across that scenario several years ago when a man from Burundi, who was in our night shelter, was suddenly granted leave to remain. It turned out that the nearest Burundian consulate was in Belgium. In order to be deported to Burundi, he needed a passport. To obtain a passport, he would have had to go to Belgium – but in order to travel to Belgium he needed… a passport! UKBA had little alternative but to let him stay.

5.   The asylum seeker is stateless. This would apply to some people from the Palestinian territories in Israel, who do not have Israeli citizenship. Since Palestine still does not have full member status

---

[71] In 2009 the Home Office attempted to deport Fatou Felicity Gaye and her four-year-old son, Arouna, to the Ivory Coast from Scotland. When they arrived in Ivory Coast, officials refused them entry. The Home Office then had no option but to bring them back to the UK pending an investigation as to what went wrong (BBC News, 29th May 2009). There have been a number of similar cases in the past few years.

at the UN, it is not a country in its own right. Therefore a Palestinian who flees abroad becomes de facto stateless. If you have ever watched Tom Hanks in *The Terminal* (our favourite family film), it's pretty much like that, except Palestinians in the UK are at least allowed out of Heathrow Airport.

6.   The country they come from keeps very poor records and can't find details of them. Many African countries, where there are millions of displaced persons and vast rural areas with little infrastructure, would be in that category. Furthermore, birth certificates are relatively rare in many impoverished countries, even in the twenty-first century – especially if you have to pay for them.[72] At the very least this lack of records will cause long delays. In some cases the country will then require some further evidence of their nationality – which the asylum seeker may not wish to give, since going back there is the last thing they want!

---

[72] According to a UNICEF report from 2007, only 2% of rural Somalians had registered their children. The figure was only 6% in urban areas. Ethiopia fared little better, with only 5% of its rural children registered. Some countries have made huge improvements in the rate of registered births, but in many countries it is still the exception.

Chapter 23
Locked up

As part of their conditional entry into the UK, all asylum seekers and other immigrants without leave to remain have to report to an immigration reporting centre on a regular basis so that UKBA can keep a check on their whereabouts. Usually this will be once a month, but it can be weekly, or even more frequently than that.

For those who have been refused asylum, this reporting can be a very traumatic experience, because the fear of being detained is ever present. Sometimes this fear can be so great that the asylum seeker simply cannot face it. They fail to report, and by doing so become 'non-compliant', and thus at even greater risk of being detained. For some, the regular visits to the reporting centre dominate their life. They do not sleep for several days as it approaches, and are deeply depressed.

When Boaz takes in new residents, one of the first things we check is whether they are reporting. That's particularly important if they are being hosted, as, in theory at least, the host could be accused of harbouring an absconder if they were not. It sometimes takes a little persuasion, but eventually everyone agrees to report. We ask them to ring us before they go in and again when they come out, so we know they are ok. Sometimes we will take them there in a car if they are particularly fearful, or have mobility issues.

As with all UKBA centres, visitors and helpers seem to be physically discouraged from coming. Dallas Court Reporting Centre is situated on an industrial estate in Salford. There are double yellow lines all around it and no parking spaces for the general public, despite the fact that traffic on that road is virtually non-existent. The nearest parking is over a quarter of a mile away in the middle of the industrial estate. Those who bring people either have to risk being clamped or drive off, park a long way away and wait for a call from their friend to say they can come back and pick them up.

Those who are still in the asylum system will have some cash, so they can travel there on public transport. If they live more than three miles away, as the crow flies, they will be eligible for a travel ticket from UKBA. Unfortunately it isn't possible to travel 'as the crow flies', as the River Irwell tends to get in the way. If, however, the claim has been refused, no help with fares is given, regardless of how far away the person lives. Boaz picks up the tab for the fares to Dallas Court, as we do visits to solicitors, hospitals and GPs. Last year it cost us £9,000 in bus fares alone, despite the fact that we don't fund social visits. If a client wants to go and see a friend, someone else will have to pay for that.

I once met a very distressed lady outside Dallas Court. Her situation sums up all that I believe to be wrong with our wonderful asylum system. She was from West Africa, had a young child of about one year, and had been refused asylum. She was living in Stalybridge, which is two bus rides from Dallas Court. According to the Transport for Greater Manchester journey planner, the quickest journey takes one hour 34 minutes. That's a round trip of more than three hours. She was required to report twice a week. She had also been electronically tagged,[73] and was subject to curfew at certain times during the week. I'm not sure how they thought she was going to abscond with a baby in tow and no money – all I do know is that all the unnecessary surveillance and endless bus journeys had brought her to the edge of sanity. Slow torture by design, courtesy of HM Government and UKBA.

Over the years the system at Dallas Court has improved, and people don't queue outside for as long as they used to. However, there is still no shelter outside, so if there is a queue, and it's raining, those who are waiting to report will get wet. Some of the staff are pleasant; others less so – or at least, that's what I hear from those who are

---

[73] As usual, Wikipedia is a mine of information. Basically, the tag consists of a chunky tag or band 'attached to the offender's ankle', which communicates with a base so that the authorities can track the offender's movements. It was originally designed to be used as an alternative to a custodial sentence for low-level criminals. More recently it has been extended to track suspected terror suspects and football hooligans. I suppose it's better than being in an immigration removal centre, but you can't escape the conclusion that, in the eyes of the UK government, asylum seekers are once again regarded as criminals.

reporting because, as a visitor, I have never been allowed in to find out.

From time to time one of our residents is 'detained' at Dallas Court. Our residents would say that 'caught' would be more like it! When the dreaded call comes into the office, emergency procedures kick in. For at least one member of staff, not much regular work will be done over the following few days.

First we need to find out all the information we can. Where and when are they being taken? Will they be taken to the short-term holding facility at Manchester Airport or straight to an immigration removal centre somewhere?[74] Does their solicitor know? If not, we get straight on to the solicitor and pray that he or she will be able to do something quickly to halt the process, though the reality is, once it's in motion, the client is very unlikely to avoid a stay in a detention centre unless they have a current fresh claim that has not been considered.

Not long ago I asked one of the local UKBA asylum team why those who are detained could not go back home under escort and pack a bag. She told me it wasn't operationally viable. Personally I think that means they can't be bothered – or they don't want the neighbours to see what they are up to. It usually takes several hours before detainees are moved from Dallas Court, so how hard would it be to escort them home so at least they have the things they need whilst in detention?

On one occasion when someone was detained, they happened to be living in a Boaz house in John Leech's constituency. John is the Liberal Democrat MP for Manchester Withington, a long-term supporter of Boaz, and now one of our patrons. He has always done all he can to help genuine sanctuary seekers who come to his advice surgeries for help. Like many inner-city MP surgeries, John's has become more and more multicultural in recent years, as asylum seekers and refugees seek help for the numerous problems they face. Unlike many MPs, however, John has been willing to openly question the asylum system and back up his convictions with action. Twice he has, with no fanfare

---

[74] AVID, the Association of Visitors to Immigration Detainees, has a list of all the immigration reporting centres in the UK and the various visitor groups that operate there. To find out how you can help in this wonderful and essential work, go to www.aviddetention.org.uk (accessed 26th February 2014).

or media coverage, joined a sleep-out in Manchester in support of destitute asylum seekers. He also took up the issue of detainees not being allowed to pack a bag with the then Immigration Minister Damian Green. The reply was not helpful, again citing operational difficulties as the excuse.

Like other procedures at Boaz, practice has improved the way we deal with detention, if not made it perfect. We now ask all clients to have a bag packed ready, in case they are detained. That way we can quickly take things to them – if not direct to Dallas Court, at least to the holding centre that evening.

The short-term immigration holding centre at Manchester Airport, or Pennine House as it is bizarrely named – it is neither a house nor anywhere near the Pennines – is in a very large, grey, industrial hanger-type building near Terminal 2. Until recently it was not on the UKBA website. I only found out the phone number through Dallas Court. Nor is it recognisable from the front of the building. The name plaque is hidden away around a corner. The first time I went there I stood in the airport staff car park barely 50 metres away from the entrance and asked three airport employees where it was. None of them knew.

The centre was recently expanded from five to 32 bed spaces. People can be held there for up to seven days before being transferred to a larger centre. If you want to visit, you have to make an appointment. Visits are for 30 minutes (including the processing time at the beginning). You are not allowed to park in the large and usually half-empty staff car park outside Pennine House, so you have to allow extra time to park in the short-stay car park at Terminal 2.

There is no visitors' reception or lounge, and no shelter outside. The entrance is on the side that never sees the sun. If the staff are busy, they will keep you waiting, whatever the weather. I was once kept waiting for ten minutes, even though I arrived five minutes late, which left me precisely 15 minutes for the visit. In 2010, during the coldest winter for many years, my colleague Nigel and his wife were kept waiting for longer than that, in sub-zero temperatures. As a result he caught a heavy cold and was off work for a week.

When you do go inside, you have to present your passport. Presumably this means that the detainee cannot have a visit from a fellow asylum seeker – even their spouse – as they will not have a passport. Then comes the body search, even down to the shoes and socks. I once asked the searcher if they had ever found anything. Of course, the answer was no.

I don't know how big the actual visiting room is. It's about big enough for three people, a little smaller than 3m x 2m, I would guess. There are no facilities – not even a water dispenser – just bare walls with a few official posters on, and a few information leaflets. It's not designed for comfort or relaxation. From start to finish, Pennine House, like Dallas Court, gives the impression that visitors are simply not wanted.

From the holding centre detainees will be taken to a larger centre, where they will be held until travel documents can be obtained and they can be deported. At least, that's the theory. In reality, most will be released at some stage because, as we have already seen, there are many reasons why people can't be deported. In addition to the ones already given, there are legal barriers. Often an asylum claim is in the process of being submitted. The solicitor completes it and sends it in, and the detainee has to be released. There have even been occasions when people have been wrongly detained because UKBA officials had failed to notice that they had an ongoing claim.[75]

---

[75] The United Nations High Commissioner for Refugees (UNHCR) set out its 'Guidelines on Applicable Criteria and Standards relating to the Detention of Asylum-Seekers' in February 1999. The Introduction starts by stating:

> The detention of asylum-seekers is, in the view of UNHCR inherently undesirable. This is even more so in the case of vulnerable groups such as single women, children, unaccompanied minors and those with special medical or psychological needs.

It elaborates on this in Guideline 7: 'Detention of Vulnerable Persons':

> Given the very negative effects of detention on the psychological well-being of those detained, active consideration of possible alternatives should precede any order to detain asylum-seekers falling within the following vulnerable categories: Unaccompanied elderly persons: Torture or trauma victims: Persons with a mental or physical disability. In the event that individuals falling within these categories are detained, it is advisable that this should only be on the certification of a qualified medical practitioner that detention will not adversely affect their health and well-being. In addition there must be regular follow up and support by a relevant skilled professional. They must also have access to services, hospitalisation, medication, counselling etc., should it become necessary.

William and their three young children. As there was no way Ruth could get off a moving train, she rang me.

I quickly told Shona what had happened. Since we couldn't take our son Caleb to his junior school that early, we bundled him into the car and headed for Joyce's house, which was about five minutes away. As we drove up we noticed a white minibus pulling away, but we couldn't see who was in it. When we arrived at the house, no one answered the door, so we assumed that the family were on the minibus and heading for Dallas Court Reporting Centre, where they would be processed before onward transportation to a removal centre.

Having lived in Manchester for more than 30 years, I have come to know a lot of shortcuts. (My wife disputes that they are actually *shorter*, and I have to confess that she is occasionally right – but only *occasionally*, mind you.) On this occasion it must have been shorter, as we managed to drop Caleb off at a friend's house and still arrive at Dallas Court before the minibus, which, as we suspected, did contain the family – or at least Joyce and the children. It transpired that William had been away from home that night.

As we were outside Dallas Court, William rang us and gave us the number of their solicitor. Eventually we were able to contact the solicitor and tell him what had happened. Later that afternoon he was able to obtain a court injunction; removal directions were cancelled and the family were returned home.

I went to the house and found Joyce and three frightened little children aged one, four and five sitting on the sofa among a pile of suitcases, clothes and other items that they had hurriedly packed that morning. The police were also there, surveying the broken front door and the glass that was all over the hallway. Apparently, when the UKBA officials had found that William was not at home, they had rung him and told him to hand himself in for deportation. His response was to tell them that if they removed his family, he would kill himself. This suicide threat was enough to warrant a full-scale search for him, and the police were sent to the house, where they broke down the door to find out if he was hiding inside. The broken door was left unsecured all afternoon, and a police car stationed outside in case he decided to come home.

Thankfully it never led to deportation, as William and Joyce's solicitor had already put in a fresh asylum claim, which is why the injunction was readily granted. Later they received refugee status, and they are now living here in safety.

There are three things to say about what happened that day. The first is that it was a phenomenally expensive operation to carry out, and proved to be a total waste of time and money. Dozens of UKBA and police staff were employed in an operation that should never have taken place, and which was paid for by the UK taxpayer.

The dawn raid team consisted of six or seven UKBA officials, some of whom were stationed behind the house – presumably in case the family tried to do a runner. Later there were five UKBA staff – four men and a woman – deployed to escort a woman and three small children to the removal centre. Several police were sent to break in to the house, and one was stationed outside the house for many hours, even well after Joyce and the children had been returned home. In addition there were five unused air tickets to Uganda, and a whole pile of administration both for UKBA and for the police. The total cost for an operation which was never necessary must have run into tens of thousands of pounds.

The second thing is that the treatment of the family was clearly inhumane. When the 'storm troopers' arrived at 6.30am, Joyce was told that there was no time to pack. Eventually she was given 30 minutes. As she had done the washing the day before, all the clothes were still wet, so she had to stuff them into plastic bags and then into suitcases along with their other belongings.

Only one of the UKBA officers who came with the dawn raid was female – a token presence, it seems, for the sole purpose of standing at an open toilet door, should Joyce need a wee. Perhaps they thought she was going to somehow escape through the toilet window past the men standing behind the house, leaving her three children behind…

At Dallas Court the family were detained in the waiting area from 7.30am until around 5.00pm, before heading off in the minibus towards the removal centre. In more than nine long hours there was very little for the children to do. They were fed sandwiches and biscuits and given water to drink. Joyce was offered no food at all. During the wait, the information given to Joyce was scanty, to say the least. For some reason she was told that they were going to be put on a ship to Holland, then on a flight to Uganda.

The call aborting the trip to the removal centre came before they had been driving for much more than five minutes, and they arrived back home around 5.30pm, where Joyce faced further questioning from two policemen about William's whereabouts. That's when I arrived amidst the chaos. Joyce and the three children were sitting, shell-shocked and silent, on the sofa, their suitcases beside them, belongings strewn around the room. There were two policemen in the hall. One was trying to sweep up the broken glass from the front door. Joyce tells me that Tosha, her eldest daughter, who is now 12, is still scared of policemen. There are no prizes for guessing why...

Thirdly, the prevention of the removal was clearly miraculous, a truly divine intervention. Consider:

1. If William had been at home, the whole family would have been taken.

2. If William had not had Joyce's mobile phone with him and inadvertently called Ruth's number, Ruth would not have received a missed call.

3. If Ruth had not rung the landline instead of the mobile, she would not have known that there had been a dawn raid.

Only by all of these eventualities happening was it possible to find out that Joyce and the children had been taken. The flights had already been booked. The family may well have been out of the country before anybody knew. At the very least they would have had to go through the traumatic experience of being held in detention.

Anne-Marie*

Anne-Marie, a young lady from West Africa, was also the victim of a dawn raid. She was living in one of our houses in Salford when three UKBA officers – two male and one female – banged on the door one morning at 6.30. Not only did they refuse to let Anne-Marie pack a bag, they did not let her keep her medication with her – only later was she allowed to have it, after a doctor had approved it. Nor were they willing to let her go to the toilet, presumably in case she tried to escape. Only when she told them that she would have to pee in the van did they relent, but she had to leave the door open with a female and a male officer watching. To compound the humiliation they tried to handcuff her on the way to the van.

Anne-Marie spent the whole day in a police cell just a few miles from her house. It would not have been difficult to allow her an extra half-hour to pack some essential clothes and toiletries, as they were clearly not in a rush to move her. It was well into the evening when she was taken to Dungavel House Immigration Removal Centre in Scotland, arriving in the early hours of the morning after several stops en route. We have since discovered that this journey is a cynical Home Office ploy to stop people interfering (even legally) with a deportation.

This is how it works: first, they detain the asylum seeker on a Friday. Then they take them to Scotland, where an English solicitor has no jurisdiction under Scottish Law, leave them there over the weekend and bring them back to England ready for deportation from Heathrow a couple of days later. It is even more effective when they choose a Bank Holiday weekend, as the solicitor might be on holiday and not contactable. By the time the client is back within his or her jurisdiction it may well be too late to do anything.

In Anne-Marie's case that meant, according to Google Maps, an overnight trip of 201 miles to Dungavel, followed by a whopping 349-mile trip to Yarl's Wood a few days later. On the way back they passed within a few miles of her home. During the journey they stopped for fuel and a break, but Anne-Marie was only offered water: they even refused to let her go to the toilet.

The fact that Anne-Marie spent two nights deprived of sleep in the back of a van demonstrates the blatant inhumanity of the UK immigration detention system. It also illustrates the flagrant wastefulness of the system, which is prepared to spend many thousands of pounds on the detention and deportation of one asylum seeker who has committed no crime in the UK.

Could it be that all this is designed to humiliate and dehumanise? Because she did not have access to her clothes, Anne-Marie ended up wearing a second-hand jumpsuit and paper knickers given to her by the staff at Dungavel House (which, incidentally, has some of the more humane staff in the detention system). It is little wonder that so many asylum detainees end up severely depressed, and some commit suicide.[76]

Thankfully Anne-Marie had a good solicitor, but we did not know whether his application for an injunction to stop the removal would be successful. Furthermore, the removal flight was the next day, so I and two of my colleagues set off down the M6 to Yarl's Wood IRC near Bedford with her suitcases, fearing that she would be deported without any of her belongings. I had also prepared some flyers so we could picket the airline check-in at Heathrow the following morning if necessary. We were halfway to Yarl's Wood when the call from the solicitor came through to say that the injunction had been granted.

Although our staff team could have turned around and gone back to Manchester when we heard the news of the injunction, we knew Anne-Marie would still need something decent to wear when she was released, so we kept going. We eventually found Yarl's Wood at the end of an industrial estate several miles from civilisation. As we only had 30 minutes before closing time, my colleagues went in to visit while I stayed with the bags to make sure they were properly dealt with. I don't know if the two staff on duty were typical detention centre employees, but I sadly suspect they were. The senior of the two, a middle-aged lady, clearly enjoyed her position of authority. She knew exactly what she had to do, but didn't have a clue about why she had to do it. She really should have had a badge with SENIOR JOBSWORTH printed on it. Her young male colleague was probably in his first week at the centre, as he clearly knew nothing at all and could only make a rather clumsy attempt to cover his lack of knowledge by grinning inanely.

---

[76] Since 2000 there have been at least eight suicides in immigration detention centres, as well as many other suicide attempts. At least five of those who died were asylum seekers. Medical Justice is a registered charity (no.1132072) that was set up in 2007. It leads the fight for adequate healthcare for immigration detainees and has exposed many shortcomings of the system in a series of well-researched, hard-hitting reports. Medical Justice deals with about 1,000 individual medical detainee cases each year. Most of this work is done by volunteers who include ex-detainees, doctors, lawyers and other experts. For more information, and to download the reports, go to www.medicaljustice.org.uk (accessed 26th February 2014).

Immediately we hit the first snag: the bags I had brought were locked, and I didn't have a key. It took Ms Important ten minutes of spluttering and mumbling under her breath about how we would have to take them back like that before she hit on the ingenious solution – after a few subtle prompts from me – of phoning Anne-Marie, as the owner of the bags, to see if she had a key. She did. But that wasn't the end of it. Although Anne-Marie's removal had been cancelled, Ms Important still insisted that she could only have 20kg of luggage. This rule had clearly been made for those being deported, and no longer applied to Anne-Marie. So I had to sort out exactly 20kg of luggage, and not a gram more, which she dutifully recorded – every single item of it – on a record sheet, which I then had to sign. It all took the full 30 minutes.

We went home, fully expecting that Anne-Marie would receive her stuff that evening and be able to sleep in some decent PJs. How wrong can you be? When she was eventually released nearly a week later, she told us that it had taken four and a half days to deliver her luggage – even though she was barely 50 metres away through two locked doors. I did think, at one point, that someone could make a really good sitcom about detention. After all, it is a farce. Unfortunately, if you're a detainee, it's not very funny.

Anne-Marie now has leave to remain and, like many refugees, is working hard and contributing a great deal to her new homeland.

Although dawn raids are less common now, they still happen, and they are still frightening for those affected. In late October 2013 the Enforcement Unit turned up at 7.00am to one of our properties. When our male support worker arrived at the house at 8.15am, there were two enforcement vans and a minimum of six armed enforcement officers there – along with an ambulance – all to arrest one middle-aged, mild-mannered Chinese lady. Her husband, whose medical records clearly indicated that he had had a heart attack in 2003 and suffered from stress and high blood pressure, ended up in hospital as a result of the trauma. Thankfully he was soon able to leave hospital, only to be detained the next day and carted off to a detention centre near Heathrow. At one point the Home Office were planning to deport the husband to Iran and his wife to China, even though they had been married for years and she had renounced her Chinese citizenship after they married. Since then the couple have been released, as often happens when they have a decent solicitor, and are awaiting a decision on a fresh asylum claim.

Leaving aside the merits of their asylum case, can someone in the Home Office please explain to me why so much force was necessary to detain one person with no history of violence? Anyone would think the lady was a suspected terrorist! And perhaps they might also like to tell the British taxpayer how much such an operation costs, since the 'hard-working British taxpayer' is always cited as the reason why we need to remove these 'illegals' who 'should not be here'.

Chapter 24
The Incredibles

Unlike the criminal justice system, under which a suspect is deemed innocent until proven guilty, the asylum system in the UK appears to assume that the asylum seeker is not telling the truth. It is perhaps understandable that an asylum seeker should have to demonstrate that they would be in genuine danger if they were to return to their country of origin, but when is it reasonable to question someone's credibility?

When Section 8 of the Asylum and Immigration Act 2004 – Credibility of Asylum Applicants – came into force, it declared that the credibility of asylum applicants would be called into question in a range of different scenarios. Saying something that is likely to 'mislead or delay the resolution of a claim'; failing to produce a passport when required; producing a false document as if it were valid; destroying a travel document without reasonable explanation – all are included as examples where credibility will be doubted.

That means that everyone who is brought in by an 'agent' will inevitably be suspected of lying, as the agent will have kept their false passport for reuse, and they will not be able to explain where it has gone. Likewise, if they have entered the country without telling Customs that their passport is false, or if they have destroyed a document because it *is* false... Most asylum seekers come from countries where possessing a false passport is punishable by imprisonment and possibly death, so they are afraid of being caught with one here. As far as I know, the Home Office has never organised mass leaflet drops on the countries our asylum seekers come from to tell them how our system works – yet there is an implicit assumption that they should somehow know before coming here.

Asylum seekers will also be considered 'not credible' if they fail to answer a question asked by a case owner or immigration judge, no matter how insensitive or downright stupid the question is: unlike criminals, asylum seekers clearly have no right to remain silent. One of the most degrading examples of insensitivity ever reported concerns the questioning – if you could call it that – of an asylum seeker who claimed to be bisexual. The interrogation, which took place without the presence of a lawyer at any time, began at 10.25am and ended at 4.00pm, with a one-hour break for lunch. It contained 220 questions, many of which were embarrassingly intimate. For the sake of common decency I will only repeat one of the questions here, namely, 'What is it about men's backsides that attracts you?' If you have the stomach for more, you will find a selection on the Free Movement website.[77]

Another 'failure' that will damage your credibility is the failure to claim asylum in the first 'safe country' you come to. Quite apart from the very generous Home Office interpretation of what is 'safe', it begs the question, 'If everyone fleeing persecution claimed asylum in the first so-called safe country, how many would come to the UK?' There are two answers to that. The less cynical answer is, 'Only those who manage to get on a plane.' The other is 'None, if the UK government can help it!' If that policy is adhered to it would lead to countries like Spain, Italy and Malta, which are the nearest to Africa, taking perhaps 100 times as many asylum seekers as we do. Hardly fair play. Definitely not cricket.

The excellent Refugee Council website[78] sums up what's wrong with Section 8 far better than I can:

> Refugee advocates remain concerned about how this Section can affect the protection of refugees. It effectively allows the Home Office to decide on an asylum case based on information about how the applicant came to the UK rather than about the merits of the individual case. This contravenes the spirit of the 1951 Refugee Convention, which clearly states that an asylum seeker should not be penalised for how they travelled to or entered a country.
>
> Section 8 also fails to take account of the fact that acutely traumatised people, especially victims of torture or rape, are generally unwilling or reluctant to discuss their experiences.

---

[77] 'Questions to a bisexual asylum seeker in detention', by Colin Yeo, Free Movement, 24th January 2014 http://www.freemovement.org.uk/2014/01/24/questions-to-a-bisexual-asylum-seeker-in-detention (accessed 26th February 2014).
[78] www.refugeecouncil.org.uk (accessed 26th February 2014).

This contradicts the UNHCR[79] handbook for asylum caseworkers, the Immigration Appellate Authority's guidance and the Home Office's own asylum policy instructions on gender issues in asylum claims, all of which clearly state that caseworkers must take this into account when interviewing asylum applicants.

This issue of credibility, then, is a key factor in asylum determinations. Lack of credibility is the single biggest reason why asylum claims are refused. It therefore stands to reason that those who make these life-changing decisions must be able to make informed judgements. They must have an understanding of the psychology of trauma and the underlying reasons for inconsistencies in accounts. Either case owners and asylum judges must be extensively trained in these issues, or there has to be sufficient legal aid in the system so that solicitors can call expert witnesses during asylum appeals. Preferably both.

It is not as if there is no background information available. The Centre for the Study of Emotion and Law[80] has published numerous excellent studies on related issues. They should be compulsory reading for those who have to make decisions on the futures of such vulnerable people.

One such study, which appeared in a periodical called *Torture* as long ago as 2006,[81] is entitled 'Should discrepant accounts given by asylum seekers be taken as proof of deceit?' The study examined the Home Office assumption 'that an account which is inconsistent is probably fabricated for the purposes of deceitfully gaining asylum status'. To do that it interviewed 43 Kosovan and Bosnian refugees – people who had *already* been granted leave to remain in the UK as part of a UNHCR refugee programme. They were interviewed twice, with interpreters.

Significantly, researchers found that:

---

[79] The Office of the United Nations High Commissioner for Refugees – www.unhcr.org (accessed 26th February 2014).

[80] www.csel.org.uk (accessed 26th February 2014).

[81] One of many excellent reports that are downloadable from the CSEL website under 'Publications'.

All [my italics] participants changed some responses between the first and second interview. There were more changes between interviews in peripheral detail than in the central gist of the account. Changes in peripheral detail were especially likely for memories of traumatic events. Participants with higher levels of Post Traumatic Stress Disorder (PTSD) were also more inconsistent when there was a longer delay between interviews.

Did this mean that they were all liars, and none were genuine refugees? Absolutely not! They were brought here precisely because they were *known* to have been victims of persecution. Yet their accounts did not tally. What this proves is that it is *very unlikely* that someone who has undergone traumatic events will say exactly the same things in two separate interviews – in fact, if their accounts are the same, it is *more likely* to have been made up! No one should be refused asylum simply on the basis of inconsistencies in their story.

The study goes on to explain the various reasons for inconsistencies. They come under two basic categories – 'Barriers to disclosure' and 'Failure to recall a traumatic event in the same way on successive occasions'.

Barriers to disclosure include:

- Not being given enough time to trust the interviewer: It is easy to understand why this is an important issue, given that most asylum seekers have a very negative experience of 'officials' in their own country, and especially of those carrying out 'interviews'.

- The attitude of the interviewer: If the asylum seeker feels that the interviewer is not sympathetic, they are much less likely to disclose information, in case it is misused. The more they are grilled, the less they are likely to reveal.

- Not trusting the interpreter: If the interpreter is from a different faith, ethnic grouping or country, they may even be seen as an enemy.

- The lack of an 'open' interview process: Leading questions can distort an account and lead to omissions. Only if the asylum seeker has the opportunity to explain things in the way they would want will the whole story be told.

- A lack of sensitivity around cultural and gender issues: Details of rape and sexual assault are particularly unlikely to be disclosed, especially to a member of the opposite sex.

Failure to recall events accurately is often caused by avoidance or shame.

Avoidance is a survival strategy that helps a victim cope with a past traumatic event. Deliberately blanking it out enables them to go on with life. It is very difficult to change this coping strategy under interview without external help. I have personally encountered this with a relative of mine who was stranded on the outskirts of Stoke-on-Trent when the car broke down. She was so stressed that, when I asked her about it a few days later, she had no recollection of the event at all. And that happened in the relative safety of the UK, not during a civil war in the Congo.

Shame is also a very powerful emotion. In our society we have little understanding of just how important it is in other, non-Western cultures. It can cause those who have been forced to betray friends and family, or been victims of sexual assault, to recall events incorrectly or partially.

The report concluded by saying, 'If the process of recognizing refugees is to be a just one, then decisions must be based on sound scientific knowledge.'

When The Independent Asylum Commission issued its final report in March 2008,[82] perhaps the most critical finding was a 'culture of disbelief' in the Home Office which led to 'perverse and unjust decisions'. When the report was published, the then Immigration Minister Lin Homer said, 'I totally refute any suggestion that we treat asylum seekers without care and compassion.' The Home Office had

---

[82] The Independent Asylum Commission ran from 2006 to 2008 and conducted a range of open consultation sessions in major cities across the UK. It produced three reports, incorporating no less than 180 recommendations. The reports, which looked at different aspects of the asylum system, were entitled 'Saving Sanctuary' (May 2008), 'Safe Return' (June 2008) and 'Deserving Dignity' (July 2008). You can find them all at http://www.independentasylumcommission.org.uk (accessed 26th February 2014).

been invited to attend and submit its evidence at all the hearings across the country but had declined to do so on every occasion. I wonder why? Were they afraid of meeting some flesh and blood people and hearing their stories? It's much easier to refuse or ignore someone you have never met. That way they are just a number among many numbers.

When I write to the Home Office about some blatantly unjust decision, the return letter frequently contains the sentence, 'We cannot comment on individual cases.' This to me seems like simply another way of saying, 'I don't want to have to justify this decision, so – no comment.' Why is it that the Home Office can get away with 'No comment', yet they insist that asylum seekers will be judged as 'not credible' if *they* ever do that?

Incredible.

Chapter 25
'Stupid is as stupid does'

'Stupid is as stupid does.' That was what Forrest Gump's mother taught him in the iconic film of the same name. It took me a while to work out what she meant, but I think it's like this: 'It's not the way you look that makes you stupid, but the things you do.'

Top of the stupid list have to be some of the questions that have been asked by asylum judges to determine whether someone is a Christian or not. Why is this important? Well, if you come from a country where Sharia Law is practised – such as Iran, Pakistan, Sudan or Afghanistan – the penalty for conversion from Islam, also known as 'apostasy', is death.[83] True, in some of those countries it is rarely carried out by the authorities, but Islamic radicals regularly take the law into their own hands,[84] knowing full well that it's very unlikely that they will ever be prosecuted for assassinating an apostate.

Likewise, if you are a Pentecostal Christian from Eritrea, you would be in serious danger if you were to return. The very least that will happen is imprisonment, usually in an underground prison with no windows, or a metal container in the desert.[85] Roasted during the day

---

[83] There is much disagreement among Muslims as to whether Muhammed taught in the Quran that apostates should be killed. It certainly teaches that Allah will punish apostates, but it is not clear if it is before death as well as in the afterlife. However, in the Hadith, which is a collection of sayings either ascribed to Muhammed or said in his presence and tacitly approved by him, there is no ambiguity: Apostasy is to be punished by death. All Muslim countries where Sharia Law is practised will therefore take that position. Among them are Afghanistan, Iran, Pakistan and Somalia, all of which contribute significant numbers of UK asylum seekers.

[84] Although apostates are rarely executed by the state due to international pressure, they are often held for lengthy periods in jail, tortured and deprived of food. If released they may become the target of Islamic militants who believe they are obliged, as good Muslims, to murder them. Stories of extra-judicial murders are regularly reported in magazines produced by Open Doors, Christian Solidarity Worldwide, the Barnabus Fund and Release International. Many are carried out by extremists like Al-Shabaab in Somalia or Boko Haram in Nigeria.

[85] See Note in chapter 4 about Helen Berhane.

and frozen at night: it's not a nice way to die. So it's quite important that the process is right when determining whether someone is a genuine convert or not.

Initially the decision will be made by the case owner. If refused, and it goes to appeal, an asylum judge will decide. If your case is based on your Christianity, the pertinent questions have to be, 'What is a Christian?' and 'How do you prove it?' Does memorising all the books of the Bible make you one? Or going to church on Sunday? Or knowing how to cook a Turkey at Christmas? (Yes, that *was* one of the questions asked at an asylum appeal.) Who can define what a Christian is? If anyone can, perhaps it's the man who invented Christianity some 2,000 years ago and who gave His name (or His title, more accurately) to it.

These are a few of the things that Jesus said about following Him. It's not exhaustive, but it's pretty clear what it's about.

Firstly, it's more than going to church once a week. Jesus constantly asked people to follow Him – and that requires commitment. He said, 'Whoever wants to be my disciple must deny themselves and take up their cross daily and follow me' (Luke 9:23, NIV). Christianity is not a soft option, as believers have discovered in countries where Islam, Hinduism, Buddhism and Communism dominate. To convert from Islam is even dangerous in the UK, as one of our former clients discovered. He was dragged off the street into a limo by a group of young Muslim men and badly beaten up – all because he had exercised his right to freedom of religion.

Secondly, following Jesus involves a change of heart and direction. That's what the word 'repentance' means. Jesus calls us to turn from sin and live righteous lives. When He began His ministry, 'Jesus began to preach, "Repent of your sins and turn to God, for the kingdom of heaven is near"' (Matthew 4:17). When someone becomes a Christian they will not stay the same. Not everything changes immediately, but they *will* change.

Gebil

Gebil from Eritrea is a good example of a man who changed when he came to know Jesus. When he first came to us at Boaz, he was depressed, ill and, frankly, neurotic. But instead of things improving, they rapidly went downhill. He stopped taking care of himself and rarely washed his clothes or shaved. When I went to see him in his bedroom, I discovered that the bed had no sheets on it, and it was the filthiest room I had ever seen. He had simply given up on life.

Not only that, Gebil was very self-opinionated, and this led to frequent arguments and even fights with others in the house. More than once the police had been called. Moreover, you could not reason with him, because you could barely get a word in edgeways. When he had made up his mind about something, you could not change his opinion. Once we even found a pickaxe handle under his bed. 'For self-defence,' he told us. We were very close to evicting him on a number of occasions.

Then Gebil began to change. He had started to attend Harpurhey Community Church, where he found acceptance and friendship. Gradually, as he listened to the preaching, he came to faith in Jesus. Prior to this he had been an atheist. It would be nice to be able to say that he was totally changed overnight, but that was not the case. He still had major anger issues, and many of his less pleasant characteristics had simply been transferred to his new faith. Nevertheless, it was clear that he was a genuine believer, not a fair-weather convert looking for a ticket to stay in the UK.

The first thing that changed was Gebil's appearance. He began to dress smartly, keep himself and his room clean and even exercise regularly. Some people didn't recognise him as the same person. His physical appearance had changed so much that the UKBA employees at Dallas Court Reporting Centre refused to accept him as the same man as was on his ID card! He also kept asking if he could volunteer – sometimes when his volunteering would not have been very helpful! The last thing that began to change was his character. Unfortunately that didn't happen before we had to ask him to leave the house, as he was still involved in frequent arguments with the other residents. We even had to bar him from the office for a while, as his visits were causing havoc.

Since he moved out, God has continued to change Gebil. He is still a work in progress, but there is absolutely no doubt that he is now a changed man – changed from the inside out by an encounter with Jesus. He has peace and purpose in his life, and a strong faith that God will be with him, whatever happens. Day by day he is becoming the man God always intended him to be. His volatile nature has calmed and softened, and we now enjoy his visits rather than endure them. We particularly enjoyed the day when he came into the office with his papers, having been granted refugee status! He is now actively looking for work, and looking to put his time and talents to good use for God and for the rest of humanity. Hopefully he will be able to go back to being an aircraft mechanic, the job he held for many years prior to claiming asylum.

Thirdly, being a Christian does not depend on how much you know. This is very clear from Jesus' encounter with Nicodemus, a member of the Jewish Sanhedrin or ruling council (John 3). Nicodemus wasn't short of *knowledge* – but he was short of *experience*. He didn't know God personally, which is why Jesus told him, 'I tell you the truth, unless you are born again, you cannot see the kingdom of God' (John 3:3). He had to have a personal encounter of the heart. Head knowledge is never enough. That's why Jesus was able to say to the thief hanging beside Him on the cross, 'Today you will be with me in paradise' (Luke 23:39-43). The thief had no time to learn a catechism, enrol on a course, or even be baptised. It was enough to be truly sorry for his messed-up life and believe that Jesus was his Saviour.

Fourthly, those who are truly Christian will want others to have that same experience. They will want to talk about their faith, and bring others to the same Saviour who has set them free. When the apostles Peter and John were hauled before the authorities for preaching about Jesus, they answered, 'We cannot stop telling about everything we have seen and heard' (Acts 4:20). No amount of threats or lashes would make them deny what they knew to be true.

So, what is a Christian? Surely it is someone who has turned from their sin, believed in Jesus as their Saviour, and has a desire to tell others. Some evidence of that will be a change in character (though that may not happen overnight), a commitment to meet with other Christians and learn more through the Bible and Christian teaching, being baptised as a sign of this repentance, and talking about their new faith.

Who is best placed to determine whether someone has genuinely converted? Is it a case owner or an asylum judge, who neither knows the convert nor, in many cases, knows what a Christian is – or is it the leader of the church that the convert attends, who can testify first-hand to their commitment and character? Surely *they* are the expert witness, in much the same way as a doctor is an expert witness when it comes to medical issues?

In 2004 the Evangelical Alliance, accompanied by Christian Solidarity Worldwide and members of City Church Newcastle, met with the Immigration and Nationality Directorate (which was renamed BIA, the Borders and Immigration Agency, and then became UKBA) to highlight concerns around asylum seekers' conversion to Christianity. Following on from that the EA began a process of collecting evidence from churches across the UK concerning Christian converts and the way their cases were being dealt with. It culminated in a Symposium on the Persecution of Christian Asylum Seekers on 7th June 2007, and a subsequent report entitled 'Alltogether for Asylum Justice'.[86]

The report highlighted a number of serious failings in determinations of an asylum seeker's Christianity. 'How do you cook a turkey for Christmas?' was by no means the only absurd question asked to establish someone's faith. Others included, 'What was the forbidden fruit eaten by Adam and Eve in the garden?' The judge concluded that the appellant could not be a Christian as his response was, 'I don't know,' rather than 'apple' – despite the fact that the fruit is nowhere identified as an apple in the Bible!

One Eritrean *Pentecostal* was asked what the name of the Pope was, as if that was relevant to him. Another was asked to name the 12 disciples. Unlike most Christians, who can't get beyond seven or eight of the 12, he named them all correctly. Unfortunately his interpreter did not know the English equivalents, and made several errors in translation. Not knowing the number of books in the Bible or identifying Jesus' birthday as 25th December (the date is unknown, but 25th December is highly unlikely to be the actual day Jesus was born) were also liable to render the appellant's testimony 'not credible'.

---

[86] 'Alltogether for Asylum Justice', www.eauk.org/current-affairs/publications/alltogether-for-asylum-justice.cfm (accessed 26th February 2014).

The document concluded by making six recommendations[87] to the BIA that would greatly have improved decision-making. As it drew near to the fifth anniversary of the report, I decided to reread it, to see if things had changed for the better. The quality of questions is perhaps no longer as bad as it used to be, and there has been some training for case owners and judges. However, genuine Christians are still not being believed, and their pastors and ministers are being ignored and even ridiculed when giving evidence on their behalf. Even when they *are* accepted as genuine converts, they are often told they can go back to their country of origin and practise their faith in secret – in other words, live a lie.

---

[87] These are the six recommendations contained in the 'Alltogether for Asylum Justice' report, which have been largely ignored by UKBA in the six years since it was published:

The Evangelical Alliance recommends that:

1. Church leaders are called as 'expert witnesses' at appeal and tribunal hearings and that the evidence they provide of the faith of a new convert is given due credence;

2. guidelines are drawn up which recognise that faith is as sensitive an issue as gender is;

3. caseworkers and adjudicators are given some basic training in the Christian faith and have an understanding that conversion is a complex psychosocial decision and not one which necessarily results in detailed Biblical knowledge or doctrinal understanding. Christians who know the appellant should be consulted in cases of conversion to verify a genuine conversion;

4. the interpreters used in interviews of converted appellants are carefully selected so that situations where the appellant is faced with an interpreter from a conflicting religious or ethnic group are avoided;

5. up-to-date and accurate country information from Christian human rights organisations is included in BIA country information reports and operational guidance notes;

6. the BIA recognises that an integral part of a living Christian faith is the willingness to share the gospel with others. Decisions about whether a convert will be safe if returned to a country where it is illegal to proselytise must take into account the fact that although not formally known as an evangelist, Christian converts will almost certainly wish to share their faith with, for example, family, friends and co-workers.

Chapter 26
'Is it legal?' – what happens when rules rule

Recently I had a heavy cold. It meant that I would wake up in the middle of the night with a very sore throat and could not get back to sleep until I had made myself a hot lemon drink. That involved waiting half an hour for the potion to do its job. I now appreciate how short-changed insomniacs are when it comes to the choice on TV. There was only so much teleshopping that I could stomach, so one night I found myself watching *UK Border Force* at 2.00am. It shows how desperate I was.

Normally I would avoid adding myself as a contributor to *UK Border Force*'s TV ratings at all costs, but at times you have to try and see things from the other side, however biased they might seem to be against those we are trying to help. On this occasion I switched on halfway through, and the programme did throw up an interesting moral issue. An officer was dealing with the case of a man whose wife and children were legally settled in the UK. He was clearly sympathetic towards the man's plight, but he turned to the camera and said something like, 'I do sympathise with him, but it's my job to apply the immigration rules, and in this case the rules say that I can't give him permission to enter.'

The British make a big deal of the fact that this is a country that believes in fair play. Hey, we even invented cricket. We don't like benefit cheats, fat-cat bankers who pay themselves millions while the economy collapses, or politicians who fiddle their expenses. Since the Tory–Lib Dem government came to power I have lost count of the number of times David Cameron has insisted that he – or they – are 'Doing the Right Thing'. The mantra seems to be highly infectious, as it has spread to his deputy Nick Clegg and ever downwards through various ministers, to the depths of the Home Office, where a succession of government spokespersons constantly use the phrase 'playing by the rules' when referring to immigrants. Shame they rarely use the same language when talking of the rich and powerful.

Another favourite Tory phrase is 'in Britain's best interests'. What this actually means is 'in Britain's best economic interests' – in other words, what will make us richer (and usually the rest of humanity poorer). A good example of this is the immigration points system. This is the system by which non-EU citizens can obtain a work permit – if they are qualified to do any of the highly skilled jobs on the list, jobs for which there are shortages in the UK.

One skillset we crave and prioritise in the points system is medical training. Over the past two or three decades the UK, which has 27.4 doctors and 103 nurses for every 10,000 inhabitants, has systematically creamed off doctors and nurses from countries like India, where there are only 6.0 doctors and 13.0 nurses per 10,000 inhabitants.[88] The fact that they have been trained at the Indian government's expense is irrelevant, because it's in 'our best interests'. In 2011 we even recruited 140 nurses from Ghana, which only has 10.5 nurses per 10,000 inhabitants – just one-tenth of the number of nurses we have in the UK. Factor in the huge difficulties of travelling through the Ghanaian jungle and the fact that Ghana only has 8,500km of paved roads compared to our 398,000km, and you will understand that those 10.5 nurses really don't stretch very far. Who knows how many Ghanaian children may have died because we stole their nearest available nurse?

It's all too easy for this island nation, cut off from the continent as it is, to keep out those whom we do not want. If the world was a playground, we would be the selfish bully in the cosy corner – the bully who makes up the playground rules to benefit himself. It is fine if the rules are good, but what happens when the 'rules' are plainly wrong and when the law does not promote justice?

One of the most frequent questions that we are asked when we do church presentations is, 'Is it legal?' – referring to the work we do with 'failed' asylum seekers. Is it legal to accommodate them? Is it legal to help them at all? At Boaz we do all we can to abide by the law: for example, we do our best to persuade clients to comply with the requirement to report to the local immigration reporting centre, and

---

[88] Taken from World Health Statistics 2010:
http://www.who.int/whosis/whostat/2010/en/ (accessed 11th March 2014).

we do not accommodate those whom we know to be deliberately evading the authorities.

But those who want to know if it's legal are really asking the wrong question. A far better question would be, 'Is it ethical?', 'Is it moral?', or, 'Is it biblical?' When St. Paul told us that 'Everyone must submit to governing authorities' (Romans 13:1), it was a call to be compliant to the general rule of law and not to be rebellious: it certainly was *not* a call to blanket obedience to evil dictators or unjust laws. The apostles were flogged because they refused to do as they were told and not preach the good news of Jesus.[89] Obadiah hid 100 prophets from the murderous King Ahab, even though he was a court official in the pay of the king.[90] The Ten Boom family and many other Christians harboured Jews in their homes when they were being hunted by the SS during the Second World War.[91] Martin Luther King deliberately ignored the segregation laws in Alabama and even handed himself in at the police station to highlight their injustice.[92] Jesus Himself broke a whole bunch of religious and secular laws when he overturned the tables of the moneylenders in the temple and drove out the merchants.[93]

All these, most of whom were martyred because of their actions, are now admired, venerated or followed by Christians today – so why are we so concerned by the idea of following their example of disobedience to unjust laws? Maybe it's because we are not prepared for the consequences. Living out the Christian faith may lead us into situations where our consciences simply do not allow us to uphold the

---

[89] Acts 5:17-42.

[90] 1 Kings 18:3-4.

[91] Corrie Ten Boom wrote, in her book *The Hiding Place* (Hodder & Stoughton, 2004) of how her family hid many Jews in their house in Holland during the Second World War in order to save them from being sent to their deaths in concentration camps. In order to feed them she had to lie, steal ration cards and obtain things on the black market – all things that went against her principles, and which she found very difficult to do. Eventually the hiding place was discovered, and Corrie and her sister Betsie were interred at Ravensbruck concentration camp. There Betsie died, but Corrie lived to tell the tale, and become one of the best-loved Christians of the twentieth century.

[92] King's stance was summed up in the statement 'everyone has a moral responsibility to disobey unjust laws'.

[93] John 2:13-16.

r of privileges: their
knowing my children,
rried ones to find a
ened there. Again, the
ead. Perhaps it has
eges while our Boaz
asic of human rights.
like I am.
the award was that it
y fears as to its lack of
he Radio Manchester
ted to interview me.
and Ethnic Minority
in a drawer with my
km run, which I think
nearly killed me. You
hn's Ambulance men
?' when you collapse

dchildren in my will. I
day – unless of course
attempt to create Big
s promise.[95] But as for
t you'll have to wait

law of the land, because that law is at odds with the way that the Bible tells us others should be treated – asylum seekers included. Hiding behind the façade of legality in order to avoid confrontation is no excuse.

hom are very
ver responded to letters I

Chapter 27
BEM

A very strange thing happened to me in Ma
picked up the mail to find a very nice, cr
addressed to me. That in itself was unusual: m
cheap manila or white envelopes. Inside was
Lieutenant of Manchester, telling me that I had
British Empire Medal (BEM) in the Queen's
asking if I would like to accept.

I can clearly remember my first reaction. I
amazement or even surprise. I was neitl
underwhelmed, so I suppose I was just 'wh
puzzled. Why would the Queen (though, of c
the dear lady herself, but rather her governm
medal? After all, I am trying to keep people in
same government wants to deport. It feels lil
'disconnect'.

My second reaction was, 'I should give
Lennon gave back his OBE, as an act of heroic
long to knock this idea on the head. Even if I di
it back, the likelihood of anyone caring would
it's a BEM, not an MBE. Unfortunately they had
wrong order. People have actually *heard* of a
Dave Smith. People know who John Lennon
though he's been dead for years. If people
usually someone else with the same name. Ther
There was even another David Smith in my clas

Empire in St. Paul's Cathedral, to a numb
children can get married in the chapel (though,
this would not be an incentive for the unn
spouse…) and their grandchildren can be chris
word 'disconnect' keeps coming into my
something to do with me being offered priv
beneficiaries are not even accorded the most
After all, they are made in the image of God, jus

If I am honest, my real reason for accepting
might generate some media interest, but sadly
newsworthiness were soon confirmed. Only
Sunday Programme, useful though it was, wa
The medal, which I proudly renamed my Blac
medal, gathered dust for the next 12 months
medals for completing the Great Manchester 1(
was probably a greater achievement, since it
know you are in a bad way when *two* St. J(
independently ask you, 'Are you alright, mat
over the finishing line.

I did think I might leave the BEM to my grar
thought it might fetch a bob or two on eBay one
there are so many BEMs floating around in th
Society that they are worth less than a politician
what actually happened to the medal… for th
until Chapter 32!

---

[94] Lennon said he was returning his MBE 'in protest agains
the Nigeria-Biafra thing, against our support of America in
"Cold Turkey" slipping down the charts'. 'Cold Turkey' w
wrote about himself and Yoko Ono coming off heroin. Pau
it down as a potential Beatles song, and it never reached h
when released by the Plastic Ono band.

[95] Of course, this does not apply to all politicians, some of
conscientious, but it certainly applies to those who have n
have sent, despite promising to do so.

law of the land, because that law is at odds with the way that the Bible tells us others should be treated – asylum seekers included. Hiding behind the façade of legality in order to avoid confrontation is no excuse.

Chapter 27
BEM

A very strange thing happened to me in May 2012. One morning I picked up the mail to find a very nice, cream-coloured envelope addressed to me. That in itself was unusual: most of my mail comes in cheap manila or white envelopes. Inside was a letter from the Lord Lieutenant of Manchester, telling me that I had been nominated for the British Empire Medal (BEM) in the Queen's Birthday Honours and asking if I would like to accept.

I can clearly remember my first reaction. It wasn't one of elation, amazement or even surprise. I was neither overwhelmed nor underwhelmed, so I suppose I was just 'whelmed' – sort of oddly puzzled. Why would the Queen (though, of course, it is not actually the dear lady herself, but rather her government) want to give *me* a medal? After all, I am trying to keep people in the UK whom that very same government wants to deport. It feels like what I would call a 'disconnect'.

My second reaction was, 'I should give it back, just like John Lennon gave back his OBE, as an act of heroic protest.'[94] It didn't take long to knock this idea on the head. Even if I *did* accept it and then give it back, the likelihood of anyone caring would be about zero. Firstly, it's a BEM, not an MBE. Unfortunately they hadn't got the letters in the wrong order. People have actually *heard* of an MBE. Secondly, I'm Dave Smith. People know who John Lennon is, or rather was, even though he's been dead for years. If people have heard of me, it's usually someone else with the same name. There are lots of us around. There was even another David Smith in my class at primary school.

---

[94] Lennon said he was returning his MBE 'in protest against Britain's involvement in the Nigeria-Biafra thing, against our support of America in Vietnam, and against "Cold Turkey" slipping down the charts'. 'Cold Turkey' was a single that John Lennon wrote about himself and Yoko Ono coming off heroin. Paul McCartney wisely turned it down as a potential Beatles song, and it never reached higher than 14 in the charts when released by the Plastic Ono band.

My third reaction was, 'What is it anyway?' In circumstances of ignorance such as this, I went to my usual fount of all knowledge. Whatever did I do before Wikipedia was invented? I should probably take out shares.

Wikipedia told me that the BEM was originally awarded either to the lower ranks in the forces for acts of bravery or to the lower classes for meritorious service to society. It was nicknamed 'the working man's gong'. Over the years the boundaries between that and the MBE became a little blurred, and in 1992 John Major abolished it, perhaps not before time, as he had obviously discovered that we no longer had an Empire. David Cameron, who clearly thinks we still do, then reintroduced it in 2012 partly in honour of the Queen's Diamond Jubilee and partly to fit in with his (laudable but probably not workable) Big Society ideas. It has become an award for service to the community, and I was one of five in Greater Manchester who were chosen to receive it.

Now I don't want to appear disrespectful, and I am truly grateful that someone, somewhere, decided to nominate me and that someone else, somewhere, ratified the nomination. I have worked hard setting up two charities, and it's gratifying to have that recognised. It's just that it seems wrong, somehow, to honour me yet treat those I represent so badly.

In the end we had a lovely family day out in October at the medal ceremony at Chetham's School of Music in Manchester. I received the medal from the Lord Lieutenant of Manchester, in the very nice setting of the Old Hall. Each award was preceded by a citation that detailed the reasons for the award. Mine was not entirely accurate. Perhaps if it had been, they might have thought twice. Afterwards we trundled off to M&S to choose takeaway meals, which we ate at my daughter Jo's house. Family, food, and a bit of fun – now that's my idea of a good way to celebrate!

When I received the medal, I was also given a large envelope (a white one, sadly, but it does have the royal insignia on the back). It contained various items of information about the award, and related offers. Medallists of the Order of the British Empire are entitled to buy (for a fee) a miniature replica CBE, OBE or MBE (being a new award they don't yet make mini BEMs). They are also entitled, for a small donation towards the upkeep of the chapel of the Order of the British

Empire in St. Paul's Cathedral, to a number of privileges: their children can get married in the chapel (though, knowing my children, this would not be an incentive for the unmarried ones to find a spouse...) and their grandchildren can be christened there. Again, the word 'disconnect' keeps coming into my head. Perhaps it has something to do with me being offered privileges while our Boaz beneficiaries are not even accorded the most basic of human rights. After all, they are made in the image of God, just like I am.

If I am honest, my real reason for accepting the award was that it might generate some media interest, but sadly my fears as to its lack of newsworthiness were soon confirmed. Only the Radio Manchester Sunday Programme, useful though it was, wanted to interview me. The medal, which I proudly renamed my Black and Ethnic Minority medal, gathered dust for the next 12 months in a drawer with my medals for completing the Great Manchester 10km run, which I think was probably a greater achievement, since it nearly killed me. You know you are in a bad way when *two* St. John's Ambulance men independently ask you, 'Are you alright, mate?' when you collapse over the finishing line.

I did think I might leave the BEM to my grandchildren in my will. I thought it might fetch a bob or two on eBay one day – unless of course there are so many BEMs floating around in the attempt to create Big Society that they are worth less than a politician's promise.[95] But as for what actually happened to the medal... for that you'll have to wait until Chapter 32!

---

[95] Of course, this does not apply to all politicians, some of whom are very conscientious, but it certainly applies to those who have never responded to letters I have sent, despite promising to do so.

Chapter 28
When the end isn't

If you are still reading, well done! You have stamina! No, it's not quite the end of the book yet, but we're getting there – just like it is for asylum seekers when they are given some form of leave to remain.

It's hard to imagine what it's like having to wait endlessly for a decision that you know will change your life. I have lost count of the number of people I have met whose lives are so focused on obtaining their papers that they simply cannot function as normal human beings in the interim. They are totally consumed by the thought that one day they will have the right to stay in the UK in safety and begin a normal life. It affects their sleep, their concentration, their health – both physical and mental – their relationships, their education. Everything appears to hinge on one piece of paper that will tell them they have leave to remain.

When someone arrives in the Boaz office waving that piece of paper, there is great celebration. There are hugs. Yes, I know there are client–staff policies and cultural taboos, but there are times when those things should be ignored. Hey, there may even be some dancing, but definitely not ballet.

It's wonderful to see the instant change that takes place when years of anxiety are lifted. Worry lines seem to disappear. Shoulders and backs straighten. Eyes light up. Of all the things I love about my job, this is the best. It makes everything worthwhile. It's why Boaz exists. Let me share a poem with you that tries to capture what it means when 'that letter' arrives.

The Letter
Today the letter came.
Today you came in to the office
with the letter,
smiling,
no longer the same.

I have seen you smile before:
not often, in the last six years of waiting,
and always wistfully,
always tinged with sadness,
always hiding the hurt beneath.

But today,
because of the letter,
your smile was wide,
your hug intense
your brow unfurrowed,
your frown unfurled,
your worry lines ironed out,
your eyes alive with light –
all because of the letter.

If only they understood
what the letter means to you,
and thousands like you.
If only they understood
why you were willing to suspend your life
indefinitely
until the letter came.

I wish I could frame your smile,
bottle your new, light heart,
capture in print your unburdened soul
and send them a copy.
Maybe then they would understand
that you are not, and never were
a number to be counted,
a statistic to be quoted,
an inconvenience to be ignored,
but a living being,
a daughter,
a mother,
a sister,
a friend,

and most of all,
a child of God.

And today,
as you smiled your freedom smile,
I could see, almost for the first time,
the image of your creator
that the letter had
at last
released.

But, if the newly granted refugee thinks their worries are over, they will be in for a very rude awakening. What they think will be the end simply isn't. Over the past few years we have begun to realise that there are still so many huge challenges to overcome, and they will not be able to navigate the choppy waters ahead on their own. The job of Boaz does not finish when someone is granted leave to remain, and we are now working hard to develop a refugee programme that will help them manage the transition from asylum to refugee status.

I can hear some of you asking the question, 'Why do they still need support? Surely that's just mollycoddling them? Shouldn't they be able to stand on their own feet, like everyone else has to?'

In an ideal world, yes, we would say goodbye and leave them to it – but I hope the following reasons will demonstrate why support is needed.

Firstly, they need support to access accommodation. When someone is granted leave to remain, they have 28 days to leave their asylum accommodation (from the date asylum was granted). Whether or not they have anywhere to go, they will have to move out. I don't know about other councils, but in Manchester refugees are now being told to access the private rented sector because there simply isn't enough social housing available. The best a single male will be offered is a place in a hostel or B&B – and often not for several weeks. In 2012–2013 we experienced a new phenomenon in our night shelters – an influx of homeless refugees who have status but nowhere to live. Thirty-eight were referred to us. The previous winter we hardly saw any.

At Boaz we often have to keep people who have been granted leave to remain until they find somewhere to live. That costs us money, and doesn't allow us to move a destitute asylum seeker into the spare room. Why is this happening? Apart from a lack of affordable private accommodation, most private landlords don't accept housing benefit. Even if they do, they require a deposit. Where is a refugee going to find a month's deposit, when they have only just started receiving benefits? Not only that, but the average waiting time for benefits to come through is currently two to three months, leaving a gap of four to eight weeks after they have had to leave their asylum accommodation when they are destitute.

In theory, this is how the process should work:

1. The refugee receives a letter saying he or she has been granted status.

2. Shortly after the status documents arrive, a National Insurance number arrives.

3. When they have a National Insurance number, they are able to claim benefits, including housing benefit (which may still take some time to be processed).

Unfortunately the reality is often very different, as delays in the system regularly lead to destitution among newly granted refugees.

We often laugh (or cry) at the inability of the Home Office to do things in the right order or at the right time, but occasionally it does work to the advantage of the asylum seeker. Our oldest resident came into the office looking very puzzled. She had been sent a National Insurance Number in the post, and had no idea why. One of the staff rang UKBA to find out, and was told that she had been granted indefinite leave to remain. They had just forgotten to tell her, or her solicitor! The papers arrived a few days later.

We have also had several clients whose names have been spelled incorrectly on their status documents. If they send them back, it takes months for replacements to arrive – months when they will be without benefits. One such case was a young Eritrean lady. She was in one of our refugee houses for five months before the correct documents arrived. During that entire time we not only had to house her free of charge but we also had to give her money to live on.

One former resident found an ingenious way of speeding things up after her name was wrongly spelled. She accepted the incorrect document and then changed her name back to the correct version by deed poll! It cost a few pounds but saved weeks of hassle! Maybe we should include a section on 'Changing your name by deed poll' in our Refugee Support Programme, as it is highly likely to happen again!

In addition to problems with housing and benefits, there are also problems accessing work. Qualifications from a refugee's home country may not be accepted here; even if they *are* accepted, they will have to pay for a statement of comparability.[96] If they have been waiting a long time for their status – some of our clients have had to wait for seven or eight years – then their skills will not be up to date. Nor will they have anything on their CV except perhaps some volunteering and some low-level educational qualifications in the UK. It will be very difficult for most people to obtain references from their country of origin, and even if they do, they will hardly be up to date – what chance is there of competing with a British or European national? It is not unusual to see refugees with a professional qualification working in menial jobs such as cleaning or security work just to make ends meet.

There is much more that could be written about the uphill struggles of refugees in the UK. Government ministers constantly harp on about the need for refugees to integrate into UK society, and I agree that they should, but it is utter hypocrisy to insist on it whilst at the same time denying them the resources needed to integrate. ESOL classes (English for speakers of other languages) have been cut to a bare minimum, yet refugees are told to learn English. When they are on Jobseeker's Allowance they are required to apply for a minimum of five jobs a week, but no one in the Job Centre is trained to deal with refugees, and understanding job adverts without good English is difficult, much less

---

[96] These can be obtained from NARIC, the National Agency responsible for information, advice, data and informed opinion on qualifications from outside the UK. The statements cost £55+ and take 10-15 working days to complete. www.ecctis.co.uk/naric (accessed 27th February 2014).

applying for them and attending interviews. The result is that refugees often have their benefits stopped because they have not applied for enough jobs. Until last year there was a government-funded Refugee Integration and Employment Service (RIES), which was administered by refugee support organisations like Refugee Action. It was there to help people in the transition to refugee status. Now it has become a victim of the funding cuts, along with advice services such as Citizens' Advice Bureaux – services that refugees had to rely on.

Sometimes, in my desperation to tell the world about asylum injustice, I dream up wacky ideas that I hope will capture the public imagination. Most of them never get beyond the drawing board, either because they are impractical or because no one has time to run with them.

I will finish this chapter by sharing one of my off-the-wall educational masterpieces with you – if only because I don't think it will ever happen in reality.

As London 2012 approached I began to think of how the opportunity could be used for publicity purposes. I came up with the *Refugee Olympics*. The idea was to hire a venue and invite the press to witness a series of short and crazy events. They were to include all sorts of things that would illustrate how ridiculously difficult it is for asylum seekers in the UK. For example:

- **Sofa-surfing or Sofa-hopping:** A very visual illustration of how many people survive homelessness. Lots of people hopping from one sofa to the next. Probably not a good idea, for health and safety reasons.

- **Running around in circles**: Every asylum seeker has experienced this, whether looking for a solicitor to take on a fresh claim or trying to find some advice or access to an English class. In this game there are no winners, because everyone gets dizzy and eventually falls over.

- **Impossibly high hurdles**: Hurdles that are so high that you can't actually jump over them – such as obtaining evidence of imprisonment in your home country when you never had an arrest warrant and no one knew where you were being held and tortured.

I don't think I ever went beyond those three, which is probably why the event never happened – but you see the idea. Since I have been working with asylum seekers and refugees, there is one phrase that I constantly hear them say – 'It's not easy.' No, not even when they are allowed to stay here.

Chapter 29
Promises, promises

Like I said before, I don't always hear very clearly what God is saying. But sometimes I do. Once or twice He has dropped something into my heart and mind that stays around and won't go away. Just so I don't forget, I write these things down. Now I have sticky-taped them to my office computer. The students who use it when I'm not there probably think I'm mad. No comment.

God's promises are vitally important, because they are like lights to guide us on our way. More often than not they are general promises that are found in the Bible, like, 'Ask and it will be given to you' (Matthew 7:7, NIV). As we act on the promise, the results come. At other times they are things that others have said, or perhaps things that have dropped into our head, as if from nowhere. Here are three that have had a massive impact on my life, on the direction it has taken, and ultimately on the work of Boaz.

The first happened many years ago. I think it was 1995, when I was still teaching and trying to build up the Mustard Tree charity from a Sunday night soup run to something more significant. My wife and I were at the Kingdom Faith Bible week in Peterborough. I went to an afternoon seminar (I can't remember the topic) and when it was ending, the leader encouraged us to turn to the next person and pray with them. I was sitting next to a lady I had never met before, and I had said nothing to her about what I was doing at Mustard Tree. When she started to pray for me, she said, 'Lord, I pray that You will take this mustard seed that has been planted, and that it will grow into a mustard tree… and that it will become an oak tree.'

Was that just coincidence? I don't think so. The reason we decided to call the charity the Mustard Tree was that the image of the birds of the air nesting in its branches conjured up the idea of a safe and secure place for the homeless.[97] It would have been encouraging enough if the lady had stopped there, but by adding the bit about the oak tree, it was as if God was adding another layer of stability, strength and permanence to what I had thought was already a pretty big vision.

The second word from God came in an all-night prayer meeting in our church building a year or two later. It was a joint meeting of local Newfrontiers churches,[98] and at one point in the evening people prayed for me and for the Mustard Tree. One of the ladies from the Stockport church began to prophesy over me. I have a lot of time for Jane's style of prophesy because it's so straightforward – and because it's pretty accurate too. She said something like this – 'Dave, God has made you like a front door to the poor and a back door to the Church.' That was it. Short and sweet – but to me, very meaningful. On the one hand, both the Mustard Tree and Boaz have as their prime objective – or 'front door', if you like – help for the poor, the most vulnerable in society. On the other hand, they are a challenge to the Church, and a way for the Church to reach out to those vulnerable groups – the 'back door'. The Church is God's answer to poverty, which I believe we are already beginning to see, and will increasingly see in years to come, as poverty hits hard in our own land. It's no coincidence that 90% of the foodbanks that have sprung up since the economic downturn are run by churches.

The third occasion was much more recent, and little more than a whisper in my ear. It was 2010. I was sitting at my desk, pondering the long waiting list of people needing accommodation, frustrated by the slow progress in obtaining houses to accommodate them, and dreaming up schemes for finding more. I think I was starting to try too hard,[99] and perhaps was losing sight of the fact that none of our

---

[97] Matthew 13:31-32 says, 'The kingdom of heaven is like a mustard seed planted in a field. It is the smallest of all seeds, but it becomes the largest of garden plants; it grows into a tree, and birds come and make nests in its branches.'

[98] Newfrontiers is a network of 850 churches across the world, of which 250 are in the UK. See www.newfrontierstogether.org (accessed 27th February 2014).

[99] John Ortberg entitled one of the chapters in his book *The Me I Want to Be* (Zondervan, 2009) 'Try Softer'. It's all about letting God do stuff in us rather than struggling to do it all ourselves. *Surrender* is probably the best word to describe it.

houses had actually come that way. They had really been gifts – from generous people, yes, but ultimately from God.

As I sat there I distinctly heard a voice in my head saying, 'I am going to give you houses.' And He has. In the last three years we have obtained seven more, taking the total to 14. None of those houses are owned by us. They have all been loaned, except a couple for which we cover the mortgage payments. When we started out I imagined we would own houses – surely that would give us more control over things? – but, actually, *not* owning them is very liberating. I also think it helps us to point upwards and say, 'This is not our doing; it's God's' – which is how it should be.

Very Green Pastures

I don't want to finish this chapter without acknowledging our very good friends at Green Pastures Housing in Southport. They are inspirational and tremendously supportive. I first came across them about seven years ago and was impressed by two things in particular. One was the size of their vision – to end homelessness in the UK. The other was the way in which pastor Pete Cunningham and others ploughed their own resources into the project to get it started and house their first homeless residents. Big vision and humble hearts – that's an unstoppable combination. I am pretty sure that's why God has honoured it so much.

From those humble beginnings Green Pastures has become a beacon of hope for thousands. There are now 36 partner organisations, including Boaz, looking after more than 485 marginalised and vulnerable people in towns and cities across the UK, from ex-offenders to former addicts and single mums – and it is growing rapidly. The homeless are being housed. Lives are being changed.

If you have surplus money and you want to invest it somewhere (apart from giving it to Boaz, which is always my number one suggestion!), then why not consider Green Pastures? The savings rate is better than an ISA, and you will know that your money is saving lives. That's surely got to be better than investing it in companies that pollute the planet or arm dictators in the third world!! Check out the footnote for more details.[100]

Some of the best ideas are the simplest ones, and if you have the heart for those who are at the bottom of the heap, God will help you find a way to help them – like He has for Boaz, and for Green Pastures.

[100] Green Pastures Housing was born in 1999, as Pastor Pete Cunningham and others from Shoreline Church in Southport purchased two flats to house homeless people. Using a mixture of faith, love and financial wisdom, it has grown year on year, initially housing the homeless in Southport and then offering to purchase houses for like-minded groups nationwide. Their dream is for every church in the UK to have at least one house to house the homeless. For more details about ways to become a partner or investing, check out their excellent website at www.greenpastures.net (accessed 27th February 2014).

Chapter 30
The 'M' word

We sing about it, dream about it, work, sweat, cheat, lie, gamble and steal for it – *Money*. When I was in my thirties I frequently worried about money, or the lack of it, and even spent a year as an insurance salesman trying to make enough to secure the future of my family. The plan was to make lots of money so that I could stop work and do lots of things for God. Unfortunately I was a lousy salesman, and the only result was a few sales of worthless endowment policies to myself and a few unsuspecting relatives. Thankfully they are a forgiving lot.

Here are a few random thoughts about money. The Boaz trustees will be rolling around the floor with laughter by now. Dave giving financial advice? Now that *is* funny! I can understand their laughter, too, as my eyes have more than once glazed over during trustee discussions on cash-flow forecasts and income deferrals. At least it will be a short chapter.

Now I appreciate that the financial systems of today are somewhat more sophisticated than they were in the days of Jesus. Judas, the disciples' treasurer, didn't have credit cards or online banking. It was strictly cash, unless you happened to have some gold around or something else to barter with. Nevertheless, I firmly believe that Jesus' pronouncements on money are just as valid today as they were 2,000 years ago, and equally valid for individuals, families, businesses and voluntary organisations.

You need money. That's about as deep as it gets, I'm afraid, and it's blindingly obvious to most. In most of the world money is the system used to exchange goods. There may be remote tribes and island communes where they have managed to do without, but you can't do much without it in the modern world, even if you would like to. Even the greenest eco-warrior has to use it sometimes. Jesus told lots of stories about money, paid His taxes, and kept a destitution fund for the poor.[101] He didn't take his disciples off somewhere and set up a hippy commune. He was living very much *in* the world, even if He wasn't part *of* it, and as a flesh and blood human being He needed money to function in the same way that you, I and Boaz do.

Because we live in a world that revolves around finance, every charity needs a proper, thought-out strategy about how much money they need to do their work, and where they think it might come from. In the last few years I have increasingly come to see that being able to deliver such a strategy means having a financing plan rather than a fundraising plan. What's the difference? Well, fundraising is built around the unknown. Applications to charitable trusts may or may not be successful. Fundraising events are dependent on volunteer support, the weather and a host of other factors. Your project is as secure as your funding, and your funding is never secure if it's all about trust funds and appeals.

Financing is something different.[102] Unlike a traditional fundraising plan, financing is an integrated, well thought-out and strategic way to help a charity raise enough money to achieve its organisational goals. It's about developing a long-term strategy for bringing enough money in to achieve the mission. It may involve some form of social enterprise, or charging for services like training or presentations. It may involve trading, or even taking out a loan. For us at Boaz, it will initially involve refugee housing.

Refugees are in desperate need of accommodation when they receive their status, but there is very little available. They also need help in the transition to independence. Boaz, with nine years of experience in housing and asylum issues, is in a good position to offer a solution that both helps people in need and is in line with our aims and objectives: at the same time, income from rents or housing benefit will make us less dependent on fundraising, even though there will always be a need for it.

---

[101] Matthew 17:24-27; John 13:29.

[102] Some useful information on financing rather than fundraising can be found on the Social Velocity website www.socialvelocity.net (accessed 27th February 2014).

Because you need money, learn how to look after it. I am still paddling in the shallow end of finance (and I'm wearing armbands). At Boaz we have some very good folk on the staff and among the trustees who understand finance far better than I do, and for that I am eternally grateful. Although a small charity can manage with some fairly basic accounting, by the time you are turning over six-figure sums you really have to have some finance-savvy people on board, because the world of the Charity Commission and Her Majesty's Revenue & Customs (HMRC) demands it. We might not like it, but we have to deal with it, and if the founders of charities can't deal with it, they need to find people who can. Amazingly, to me at least, there *are* people who revel in the accounting world. They are worth their weight in gold – or pounds, if you prefer.

Don't let money run your life or your business. Jesus summed it up by saying, 'You cannot serve both God and money' (Matthew 6:24). Money is of itself neutral, just like the internet or TV – neither good nor bad. What makes it good or bad is how we use it and the value we place on it. Charities and even churches can be sucked in to chasing after finance so much that they forget what their mission is. Mark's gospel tells the story of a rich young man who came running up to Jesus and asked Him what he needed to do to inherit eternal life.[103] Rich though he was, he clearly knew there was something missing in his life. Neither his wealthy lifestyle nor his outward religious obedience could satisfy a deep inner longing. To others he seemed to have it all, but in fact he was miserable because he couldn't break free from the shackles of wealth.

I once met a guy just like him. He was a middle-aged, successful businessman with a lovely house in the country and a nice family. He turned up unannounced one day in the dingy basement of Youth Action Hull, where I was the temporary coordinator, and he offered to do some volunteering. He began to pour out his soul to me, then a 22-year-old who was still decidedly wet behind the ears. Materially he had everything, but something was still missing. I don't know if Jesus would have given him the same advice that He gave the rich young

---

[103] Mark 10:17-31.

man in Mark's gospel, but I suspect it would have included something about giving away his wealth as well as becoming a follower.

Charles Dickens caricatured the misery caused by hoarding wealth in the person of Ebenezer Scrooge in his 1843 novel, *A Christmas Carol*. In it Scrooge changes from being a stingy and dislikeable old man to a joyful philanthropist who can't wait to find needy people to give his money to. It brings to mind Jesus' parable of the rich fool who stored up wealth for the future but died before he could enjoy it.[104] Simply put, you can't take it with you when you die, so you might as well give it away while you can. If you do, you'll be much happier for it, knowing that it's being put to good use helping others. Like Scrooge, breaking the shackles of wealth will liberate your soul. As the Bible says, 'God loves a cheerful giver' (2 Corinthians 9:7, NIV).[105] Apparently the Greek word for *cheerful* can also be translated as *hilarious*. Laughing all the way *from* the bank. I love it.

By the way, if you need any suggestions about where to put your money, do give me a ring...

Don't worry about it. One of my favourite Bible passages is found in chapter 6 of Matthew's gospel, starting at verse 19. It's all about money, possessions and the stuff we need to live, like clothes, so it's very practical, and applies to everyone. I like to visualise *how* Jesus might have said things, as well as hear *what* He said, and when He says, 'Can all your worries add a single moment to your life?' (verse 27) I imagine a wry smile on His lips. It's one of the greatest truths there is, yet so few people have discovered it: *there is absolutely no point in worrying about anything, because worrying can never solve the problem!* If I am 1.5m tall, worrying about it will not make me 1.8m. If I can't do maths, worrying about it will not turn me into Einstein. If I am ill, worry will not cure me; if anything it will make things worse because it can affect sleep, digestion, concentration and a host of other things.

---

[104] Luke 12:13-21.
[105] Verses 6-7 say, 'Remember this: whoever sows sparingly will also reap sparingly, and whoever sows generously will also reap generously. Each of you should give what you have decided in your heart to give, not reluctantly or under compulsion, for God loves a cheerful giver' (NIV).

Worry is not the same as concern. People who are not concerned about bad things are lacking in care and compassion. Concern may drive you to find a solution, whereas worry tends to focus too much on the problem. Not being concerned about things should, er... concern us.

I can hear some people saying, 'Ok, smarty-pants, it's all very well saying I shouldn't worry, but how can I stop?' Jesus did not leave us in the lurch. The answer to worry is right there in the passage. It's knowing that we have a heavenly Father who cares for us:

> These things [the cares of the world] dominate the thoughts of unbelievers, but your heavenly Father already knows all your needs. Seek the kingdom of God above all else, and live righteously, and he will give you everything you need.
> *Matthew 6:32-33*

If God really cares about us, He will provide for us. That doesn't mean we can sit back and do nothing (the Bible also has a lot to say about laziness), but it does mean that if we do what He suggests – seek to please Him and live righteous lives – then He will keep His part of the deal and give us what we need.

That's true of individuals, and it's true of charities like Boaz – it's the added faith dimension that enables us to trust God when we can't see an answer to a problem. It's what keeps us going. It's also the reason that money and gifts often come at unexpected times from unexpected sources: twice Boaz has received large donations out of the blue just a few weeks before the end of the financial year, without which we would have made a financial loss. And it's the reason why we should never have to worry about the future. Like Jesus said, probably with another wry smile and a twinkle of the eye, 'So don't worry about tomorrow, for tomorrow will bring its own worries. Today's trouble is enough for today' (verse 34).

Chapter 31
Solving asylum

Solution 1 – Imagination

The older I get, the more I realise how little I know, and how much more there is to learn about the world, God and people. That's why heaven won't be boring. Just like the universe keeps expanding, so will the things we can do and learn. (And I have some folk to search out, too, with a few burning questions. That could take a while!) We have an infinite God, and when we finally meet him face to face, there will be an infinite number of wonderful things to do to fill the time – assuming, that is, that time will still exist. Hardly a week goes by without the discovery of a new species somewhere on Earth, and we've hardly begun to explore the oceans, where there are myriads of life forms, all totally amazing. God is astoundingly imaginative, and He has equipped us, who are made in His image, with the ability to be imaginative too.

I have come to the conclusion that one of the greatest problems with the world is lack of imagination. As a race we have forgotten how to use the God-given ability to think laterally, to solve problems creatively, to live 'outside the box'. It's a malaise that affects the Church to a large extent, but in my experience it has been nowhere more endemic than it is within the institution of the Home Office. It's not so much that the decisions made by UKBA case owners and immigration judges are without logic, but rather that they seem unable to imagine what it is actually like to flee from persecution and war. Judges who grew up in the leafy English countryside and have no experience of being falsely accused, detained without cause or tortured, do not seem to have the capacity to imagine what it might be like for those who *have* been. Sitting in the safety of an English courtroom, it is easy to reflect on what people perhaps ought to have done in a certain situation, had they been able to think rationally. It's quite another matter to be there in that situation with a hundred thoughts flying through your head and trying to figure out what to do next, yet having no time to figure out anything much at all.

Over the years I have heard and read many stories. If I had my time again, I would have kept far better records, but I never knew at the time that I would need them for a book. It may be that these recollections are not 100% accurate: I may even have combined a couple of cases – but it doesn't matter, because they are here to serve as illustrations of a lack of imagination.

One of our Zimbabwean residents had a husband who was in the opposition MDC party. One night a gang of Zanu-PF Youth League members (Mugabe's equivalent of the Hitler Youth) came calling. They dragged the father and son away and murdered them. The wife, who witnessed the events, was asked by the case owner how many thugs there were. Because she said she didn't know, she was deemed to be 'not a credible witness'. At that precise moment I don't think mental maths would have been her top priority. Whether there were eight or ten was of no importance, yet it clearly was for her case owner. Later the lady's refusal was overturned, and she now has leave to remain in the UK.

A young Sudanese man who joined a rebel group was captured by the Sudanese Army and held in an army camp along with several others. The camp was attacked by rebels at night, and the prisoners all made a run for it as shells exploded around them and bullets whistled over their heads. The young man's story was not believed because he was not able to identify any of the dead and wounded bodies that he ran past. Was the judge not able to picture the darkness, the smoke, the confusion, the panic? Was he unable to imagine his overwhelming urge simply to be a survivor?

A young girl, born in Ethiopia of Eritrean parents, was left behind when her parents were deported to Eritrea during the war between those two countries. For a while she was able to continue her studies, but eventually had to hide for fear of the authorities. She was refused asylum on the grounds that, if she had been in real danger, she would have left the country earlier. I have five children, the youngest of whom is in his mid-teens. You would think, after five, that I would have sussed the way teenage brains work, yet I still have no idea. Even when in a safe and loving environment, teenage behaviour is not always rational, so why should we expect a girl living in a war zone, with no stabilising parental influence, to be able to work out the optimum time to flee the country?

Without imagination, you cannot have empathy. Without empathy, you will not have justice.

Solution 2 – Scrap it and start again

As I mentioned earlier, I am involved in the Still Human coalition. Since its inception some five years ago it has worked very hard, under the very able leadership of Mike Kaye, to end destitution among refused asylum seekers through lobbying, campaigning and engaging with UKBA around four major issues:

- Support for all destitute asylum seekers until they are either granted leave to remain or removed from the UK

- Free access to healthcare for all asylum seekers while they are here in the UK

- Permission to work if their case has not been resolved within six months

- Improved decision making

There have been some successes, notably in decision making, so the coalition has definitely been worthwhile. The rate of initial decisions now being granted leave to remain is 36% – higher than at any time since I have been working with asylum seekers. Primary healthcare is available to all, and there have been other important improvements in healthcare entitlements too.

On the issue of work there has been absolutely no movement, despite significant support in Parliament as well as from Boris Johnson, the Mayor of London, and from the CBI (Confederation of British Industry), who are very well aware of the net contribution that refugees make to our economy.[106] It seems our political leaders feel

---

[106] Refugee Council ran a Let Them Work! campaign in conjunction with the TUC and Student Action for Refugees (STAR) in 2008–2009. One hundred and seven MPs signed the Early Day Motion (EDM) 960 calling for asylum seekers to be allowed to

that allowing asylum seekers to work would undermine the whole system.

Maybe that's precisely what needs to happen.

My question is this: how long will it take, nibbling away at the injustices of the system, for change to come? I understand that there are few other options at the moment, but the bottom line is that the current system is incapable of delivering justice for everyone because, at its heart, the system itself is deeply discriminatory and unjust. It simply has to be scrapped. We have to start with a blank sheet of paper. Whether our politicians have the courage to do something quite as radical as that is doubtful, but that is what we have to demand.

I am often annoyed by people who whinge about the local council, their MP or the government. Complaining is fine, but I rarely hear anyone offering a constructive alternative. So in order to avoid being hypocritical, I guess that's what I now have to do. So here goes: 'Dave Smith's Alternative Asylum System'. It won't be perfect, and I'm sure some of you will find some obvious flaws in it, but one thing I will absolutely guarantee – it will cost far less than our current system, saving millions of pounds in taxpayers' money.

The Radical Alternative Asylum System

1. **Take the system out of the hands of the Home Office and make it independent of government**: Set up an Asylum Commission to appoint an Asylum Board to not only oversee the decision-making process but also to devise the process itself. Board members could be MPs representing the main parties, but also others from the charitable sector with expertise of asylum. Above all, it must be neither an arm of government nor offered up to the highest bidder from the private sector.

2. **The initial interview:** To replace the current screening interview, after arrival an interview is conducted that simply aims to ascertain basic information about the asylum claimant – their

---

work whilst their claims are being considered. Boris Johnson and the CBI both lent their support. For economic benefits see Note 35.

name, age, country of origin and basic reason for claiming asylum. It must be:

- Brief (to avoid unnecessary trauma)

- Carried out by someone of the same sex in civilian clothes, in case the claimant has suffered abuse at the hands of people in uniforms in their own country

- Never used to determine credibility, and not admissible as evidence at a later stage, as they have no access to a solicitor at this stage and are unfamiliar with the UK asylum system

3. **Initial reception phase:** After claiming asylum in the UK, the claimant is given a room in a reception hostel. Unless there is compelling reason to believe they might be a threat to the country, they should *never* be locked up. The initial period in the hostel should be at least a month to ensure that they fully understand the system. (At the moment no one really understands the system, even when they have been through it and come out destitute the other end, because no one takes the time to tell them how it works. A minor omission on the part of the Home Office, methinks.) Each dispersal area has reception accommodation so that there is no need to move out of the area later. This would avoid having to change solicitor (or travel hundreds of miles to London when they need to see their solicitor!).

4. **During the hostel phase:** The claimant is:

- Introduced to volunteer befrienders, who help them orientate and navigate the system

- Given English lessons if needed

- Given a full explanation of the system – this could be done with the aid of an interpreter, or perhaps by video in their language

- Given access to a solicitor, who will advise and work on their case whilst they are in the hostel. Legal aid would be heavily front-loaded to enable the solicitor to present the case fully at the substantive interview.

5. **After four weeks there is a 'substantive' interview:** At the interview they are represented by their solicitor, and may also have their befriender or other friends present. The interview is inquisitorial – not, as at present, adversarial. There is no Home Office respondent present, asking awkward questions and pouring doubt on the claimant's credibility. A panel of three trained independent adjudicators hear the evidence as presented by the asylum seeker, with the aid of their solicitor. Witnesses may be called. The aim is simply to establish the basis for their asylum claim.

6. **After the substantive interview:** The adjudicators make a decision based on what they have heard at the interview. They would have three options rather than the current two. They can:

   - **Grant leave to remain:** If they are convinced that the claim is genuine they can give leave to remain in the UK. Leave to remain will NEVER be less than five years; anything less than this discriminates against the asylum seeker when it comes to education and work. Currently many asylum seekers are given two and a half years, which means they cannot access higher education courses, and employers will rarely offer them a decent job.

   - **Defer the case for further evidence:** This is *not* a refusal. It simply gives the claimant and his or her solicitor more time to find fresh evidence.

   - **Reject the claim:** If they are convinced that it is unfounded, the claim can be rejected – although the claimant should always be believed unless there are compelling reasons not to. If we get it wrong, I'd much rather we let someone in who was not in danger of persecution than return someone to the risk of torture or death.

4. **All refusals would automatically come with one right of appeal:** Appeals and deferrals should happen at least two months after the

initial decision, to ensure sufficient time for the solicitor. Solicitors can also request an extension if they can demonstrate good cause.

5. **After the initial month in the hostel:** The asylum seeker is moved into asylum accommodation, preferably in the same locality where they already have links with befrienders and a solicitor.

6. **After six months they have the right to work, whatever their status:** This could save millions of pounds in asylum benefits each year.

7. **If asylum seekers commit a crime:** They are to be subject to the same process as other criminals. If convicted, they are liable to go to prison, just like anyone else. Deportation should be an option, but not if the likely treatment in their home country is going to be inhumane. If we treat them better than they deserve, they are much more likely to reform and become better human beings.

8. **Those who are about to be removed:** Someone can be detained for a maximum of one month, during which time the Home Office must arrange documents and the flight. If they have not been removed during that time, the Home Office can apply for an extension, but must prove imminent removal, otherwise the detainee must be released. The bail system,[107] which is frankly haphazard and arbitrary, should also be radically overhauled: if release is compulsory, and refused asylum seekers are still accommodated until removal, there is no need for bail.

---

[107] To understand the bail system in the UK (as much as anyone *can* understand such a ramshackle process), it is well worth reading the BID (Bail for Immigration Detainees) report 'A nice judge on a good day', July 2010, downloadable at http://www.biduk.org/420/bid-research-reports/a-nice-judge-on-a-good-day-immigration-bail-and-the-right-to-liberty.html (accessed 11th March 2014). A more recent but equally damning report is 'Immigration Bail Hearings: a Travesty of Justice?' which you can download from http://closecampsfield.wordpress.com/?s=Immigration+Bail+Hearings%3A+a+Travesty+of+Justice (accessed 11th March 2014).

I am sure someone could improve on my ideas, but even as they stand they would save a lot of money in unnecessary appeals, judicial reviews and cancelled flights; they would keep people out of jail who are not criminals, greatly reduce mental health problems and, best of all, perhaps give some credence to the notion that the United Kingdom is a fair and just country.

Chapter 32
Time to act

This book is growing longer by the day – and it's all the government's fault, because they keep making daft proposals which make me angry, and then I have to write about them. I don't anger easily, but right now I'm spittin' feathers, and the staff in the Boaz office have earache from my mutterings and deep sighs.

The Immigration Bill 2013,[108] which the Home Secretary Theresa May has said is designed to 'create a really hostile environment for illegal migrants',[109] is the latest in a line of cruel measures that seriously affect the lives of those seeking asylum. It includes plans to cut legal aid even further, introduce a new 'residence test', force landlords to carry out immigration checks on their tenants, and make it harder to access healthcare.[110] It is currently zooming through

---

[108] The Immigration Bill was introduced into the House of Commons on 10th October 2013. Subject to its Parliamentary progress, the bill is expected to receive royal assent in spring 2014. According to the government's own statement:

> The bill will reform the removals and appeals system, making it easier and quicker to remove those with no right to be here. It will end the abuse of Article 8 of the European Convention on Human Rights – the right to respect for private and family life. It will prevent illegal migrants accessing and abusing public services and the labour market.

[109] This idea was first mooted in an interview in the *Daily Telegraph* in May 2012: http://www.telegraph.co.uk/news/uknews/immigration/9291483/Theresa-May-interview-Were-going-to-give-illegal-migrants-a-really-hostile-reception.html (accessed 11th March 2014), and reiterated when the Immigration Bill was introduced in October 2013: http://www.theguardian.com/politics/2013/oct/10/immigration-bill-theresa-may-hostile-environment (accessed 11th March 2014).

[110] Rosa Crawford from Migrants' Rights Network wrote on 18th October 2013:

> Preventing migrants from using the health service will endanger public health and cost the NHS even more at a time when it is already reeling from having to make £20 billion efficiency savings.
>
> Importantly, the Immigration Bill will also ramp up the level of discrimination against anyone who doesn't 'look' or 'sound' British. These are most likely to be subject to document checks, as we wrote our submission to the Department of Health plans to charge migrants to use the

Parliament at an abnormally alarming speed, and likely to become law before this book is printed (I was going to say 'makes me rich' – you can but dream). I am praying desperately that the Lords, some of whom have no political axe to grind and may therefore act out of conscience rather than anti-immigrant populism, will have the guts to throw out or water down the bits that are nasty – which is most of it.

Interestingly – and, some would argue, very amusingly – the Bill has already caused one casualty: not an asylum seeker, but the Immigration Minister Mark Harper, who 'fell on his sword' on 7th February 2014, as the Bill had just passed through the commons. He felt he had to resign because he discovered that his cleaner was in fact an illegal immigrant. The *Guardian* reported:[111]

> Correspondence between Harper and Cameron, published in a *Spectator* blog, reveals that on 7 February Harper wrote to the prime minister explaining how he had tried on several occasions to make sure his cleaner had leave to remain in the country. When appointed in September 2012, Harper repeated the background checks into his cleaner, whom he has hired since April 2007.

I wonder if Mr Harper's faux pas will make the noble Lords realise that at least one part of the Bill is utterly nonsensical: if an immigration minister, with all his connections and supposed knowledge of the immigration system, cannot discover that his own cleaner is an illegal immigrant during the five and a half years that he employed her, how on earth can he – or his superiors – expect ordinary people like landlords and hospital staff to accurately check on the immigration status of those they are dealing with?

NHS . The Runnymede Trust has already shown there is racial discrimination in the housing market, and this Bill will only make the situation worse. No wonder Shami Chakrabarti , director of Liberty, called it a 'race relations nightmare'.

A full briefing on the Bill can be found at http://www.migrantsrights.org.uk/files/publications/MRN-Immigration-Bill-briefing-Oct-2013.pdf (accessed 11th March 2014).

[111] http://www.theguardian.com/uk-news/2014/feb/09/mark-harper-immigration-minister-resigns (accessed 27th February 2014).

The proposals in the Bill are worth an entire book, but I won't waste my time on them, because the mere fact that the government is even *considering* them has exposed the naked truth. The Emperor really never had any clothes, and if 'Big Society' ever was a sincere attempt at giving power to the people, it certainly didn't include asylum seekers or the NGOs helping them, all of whom are totally opposed to the provisions of the Bill.

If these plans come into effect, refused asylum seekers will not be able to put in fresh claims unless they can pay for them. They may not even be eligible for primary healthcare, and the strain and stress they suffer will be multiplied a hundredfold. I do not need to be a prophet to know what the results will be.

People will suffer and even die from preventable diseases, or freeze to death sleeping on the streets in winter. Others will lose the will to live, and commit suicide. That already happens, particularly among those held in detention,[112] but I would expect the number taking their lives to rise sharply. The strain on charities, local councils, hospitals and police will be compounded, and it will cost us all far more to deal with the fallout from these measures than they will ever save in penny-pinching.

I am not one for jumping on every demonstration bandwagon. In fact, in my first 64 years of life I have only participated in three events that could be called demonstrations – but that has begun to change. At the start of July 2013 I took part in a very peaceful and positive rally asking for 'Dignity not Destitution' for asylum seekers. Two weeks later I joined around 250 people to protest against the proposed legal aid cuts. I have never seen so many suits and high heels at a demo! Lawyers are appalled at the dismantling of one of the pillars of the welfare state that has given poor people the same opportunity as the rich to seek justice in court.

Unless there is a drastic change in policy, I suspect it won't be the last demo I attend, because I can see no end to the current obsession with trying to drive immigrants out of the country. It is difficult to reach any conclusion other than that those in power are doing this in

---

[112] Of the eight suicides in immigration detention centres since 2000, at least five were refused asylum seekers.

an attempt to appease right-wing xenophobes who are defecting to UKIP, and to ensure that the readers of certain tabloid newspapers are kept onside in the run-up to the next General Election.

When the Conservatives came to power, David Cameron began to talk about his vision of 'Big Society', where everyone, irrespective of their status, had a part to play in mending a broken society and contributing to the future agenda for the country. In many ways his speech on 19th July 2010 was innovative and exciting. He talked of 'a whole new approach to government and governing', and a radical shift away from centralised, top-down government. It was a speech to arouse hope for the future.[113]

While I have a natural scepticism about 'compassionate conservatism', I took the Prime Minister at his word. I began to engage in government consultations and offered suggestions as to how we could save money without cutting services. But as I delved more and more into the realities of what was on offer on the asylum front, more and more barriers emerged. We looked at the possibility of setting up a work club for new refugees, until we realised that it would have to be done with absolutely no funding input at all. We looked at the possibility of taking on government contracts for asylum housing, until it became evident that only organisations with a massive capacity would be in a position to bid for them. The contracts went to three multinationals. So much for grass-roots involvement.

I have come to realise that, however well-intentioned Big Society is, in the asylum sector at least, government has absolutely no intention of taking its hands off and allowing those on the ground to contribute to the decision-making process. No one has been listening, let alone responding to those working with the disadvantaged and vulnerable. The gap between the rhetoric of Big Society and its implementation is wider than the Grand Canyon.

Just in case you think I have turned into a bitter old man who just complains about everything, I want you to know that I spend a lot of my time trying to engage with those who appear to be on the other side, and I will continue to do so for as long as I am able. I don't want

---

[113] You can find a full transcript of the speech at
www.gov.uk/government/speeches/big-society-speech (accessed 27th February 2014).

a war if there is another way. Nor do I like slinging mud at people because, when you do that, it tends to end up on the slinger as well. You can't change an opinion unless you talk to the one who holds it, however wrong you think that opinion is.

That is why, at Boaz, we don't just do Social Action – we are heavily involved in calling for Social Justice as well. It has taken a long time, but the Evangelical Church has just begun to realise that speaking up for those who have no voice is just as much a part of the gospel as is evangelism or helping the poor. The Church is very good at offering help – just look at the explosion of foodbanks across the country – but how many are challenging the widening gap between the haves and have-nots which has led to the need for those foodbanks? As it says in Proverbs 31:8-9:

> Speak up for those who cannot speak up for themselves; ensure justice for those being crushed. Yes, speak up for the poor and helpless, and see that they get justice.

Over the past few years I have become increasingly involved in coalitions, movements and networks. Some are well established, such as Still Human. Others are in their infancy. Some are very small, addressing particular issues, like a group of Christians meeting to address the issue of Christian converts being refused asylum. For me, perhaps the most exciting prospect is the possibility of bringing together all those in the asylum world who want to see change in a sanctuary summit – a mass demonstration calling for justice and compassion for those seeking sanctuary in the UK. This would involve all the key refugee networks and organisations, bringing together those from the City of Sanctuary movement, NACCOM, the Detention Forum,[114] Still Human, the Churches Refugee Network, etc. On our own we are easily dismissed. Together that will not be so easy.

A few chapters ago I mentioned my British Empire Medal and my reluctance to accept it because of the way asylum seekers are treated here. With the advent of the Immigration Bill I felt I had no choice but

---

[114] The Detention Forum is a loose network of more than 30 NGOs who are working on immigration detention issues. See www.detentionforum.wordpress.com (accessed 27th February 2014).

to return it in protest at the increasing persecution being perpetrated by the government. I returned the medal in October 2013, along with a letter to the Prime Minister, with which I conclude this chapter. Ten days later I received a reply from an unnamed member of the PM's staff, telling me that it has been passed on to the Home Office, as the PM feels they are better placed to deal with it. Make of that what you will, but I know from past experience what that means – at some point, when it has been passed down the line to a very junior member of UKBA staff, I will receive a reply – cut and pasted from standard government policy documents. So far (at the time of going to print) I have only been waiting six months.

But the truth is, even if I never receive a reply, I actually did it for *myself* more than anything else. I feel much lighter now. Funny how such a small thing can weigh so much.

> Dear Mr. Cameron,
> Last year I was awarded the British Empire Medal for Services to the Community. At the time I was slightly bemused at the award, since my current charity work as Director of the Boaz Trust is providing accommodation and support for asylum seekers who have been refused asylum here, but not been returned to their country of origin. Nevertheless I was grateful that I had been nominated and that my charity work had been recognized, so I accepted the award. I hoped that it might provide an opportunity to highlight the immense difficulties faced by those we are helping: I also accepted it in good faith as a sign that your vision of Big Society was indeed a vision where all, from the top to the bottom, would be able to play their part in renewing and reviving the country we live in.
>
> One year later I have come to realize that the promise of an integrated society where all are valued and all can contribute is, at best, an ill-conceived dream. I understand the need for some form of austerity, but am appalled that those expected to fill the financial black hole are the weakest and most vulnerable in society, whilst those who have caused it and those who could lose half their wealth without noticing have remained untouched.

Since the first mention of Big Society I have responded to several government consultations and ministerial challenges to save money. I even wrote a long letter to Damien Green when he was Immigration Minister, outlining six ways to save money and also deliver a fairer asylum system. Almost all the recommendations were taken from *Asylum Matters*, a report produced by the Centre for Social Justice. Mr. Green never replied, despite promising to do so, and none of the recommendations have been implemented. It is very clear that those on the front line, who are picking up the pieces caused by the austerity measures, are not being listened to. Charities and voluntary groups are expected to fill the gaps, but government policies are making the gaps ever wider. Like the Israelite slaves in Egypt, we are expected to make bricks for the empire, but government now refuses to provide the straw for the bricks.[115]

Recent proposals for a new residence test, landlord immigration checks, further legal aid cuts and reduction in healthcare leaves me in no doubt, Mr. Cameron, that your government considers those seeking asylum to be of less worth than other human beings, and for this reason I am returning my British Empire Medal. Below I have, for the sake of brevity, outlined five ways in which asylum policy in the UK contravenes human rights and is out of kilter with other forms of law and justice in the UK. I appreciate that some of this is inherited from an equally culpable Labour government, but that is no excuse.

1. From the very start of the asylum process those seeking asylum are not accorded even the same rights as those accused of criminal offences in the UK. Even though the system is adversarial, like the criminal justice system, they are not given a solicitor until after the substantive

---

[115] The story of how the Egyptian taskmasters forced their Israelite slaves to produce the same amount of bricks so that Pharaoh could continue to build his Empire, yet without giving them the resources to do so, is beginning to sound eerily like what charities and voluntary groups are being asked to do in the Big Society. You will find the story in Exodus 5:6-21.

interview. Nevertheless the Home Office frequently refers to the appellant's statements from both the substantive and even the screening interviews in order to cast doubt on their credibility, leading to many unjust refusal decisions.

2. Unlike the criminal justice system, where the defendant does not have to prove their innocence, in the asylum system the claimant is required to prove their claim. This is often impossible to do because those who are guilty of persecuting them rarely admit to it or document it, and the asylum system allows neither enough time nor legal aid to gather the evidence, even if the evidence is available.

3. Although they have committed no crime, many asylum seekers are locked up in Immigration Removal Centres with no idea of how long they will be held there. This often applies even if they cannot be returned to their country of origin. These centres are administered by multinational private companies, some of whom, like G4S, have appalling records both of incompetence and human rights abuses. Since 2000 there have been 8 suicides in immigration detention, and hundreds of suicide attempts. The whole policy of UK asylum detention is contrary to the spirit of the UNHCR guidelines on detention, particularly Guideline 7, and the courts have frequently upheld claims of unlawful detention.

4. The UK asylum system often fails to comply with the requirements of the UN Convention on Refugees. Article 31 of the 1951 Refugee Convention prohibits states from penalising a refugee for illegal entry when the purpose of their entry is to claim asylum, yet asylum seekers are frequently imprisoned in the UK for entering the country on a false passport.

5.   Article 8 of the ECHR states that 'Everyone has the right to respect for his private and family life, his home and his correspondence'. In the past thirteen years since I first encountered asylum seekers, I have come across countless example of the Home Office blatantly ignoring this human right, deliberately seeking to divide families and returning vulnerable people to situations of extreme danger.

Mr. Cameron, you recently praised the contribution of the Christian church in this country. One of the major tenets of faith that all Christians agree upon is Christ's command to 'do to others what you would have them do to you'. It is my prayer that those in government would allow themselves to imagine what it is really like to flee from countries ruled by evil dictators and lands where human rights abuses are endemic. Until they do so there will never be a just asylum system in this country.[116]
Yours Sincerely

Dave Smith, BA.

---

[116] There are many much weightier critiques of the UK asylum system than mine. The best I have found so far is Frances Webber's *Borderline Justice* (PlutoPress, 2012). It takes the lid off the UK asylum system, in the process uncovering what can only be described as a deliberately hostile and overtly racist system designed to keep genuine refugees out of the UK. I thought I knew how badly refugees were treated: this book has made me realise that the truth is far worse than I ever dreamed.

Chapter 33
Family Night

One of the privileges of working with asylum seekers is that they teach you so much. Life at Boaz is a constant learning process, often a result of things our clients have said or done. One such 'educational moment' came in 2012.

I don't normally deal directly with clients any more: we have some fantastic, dedicated, specialist staff who do that now. In fact, I no longer know all the residents in our houses, much less their stories. I miss the relationships I used to have, but campaigning and networking has been a necessary part of the development of Boaz. Just occasionally, when there is a staff shortage, I do some face-to-face client work. This was one of those times.

For some reason that I no longer recall, on this particular day I was the only one in the office with a car. One of our clients, a young lady, had a very important hospital appointment, and though we would normally send a female member of staff, this time I was the only one who could do it.

At this point I need to fill you in with a little bit of background. The young lady concerned was barely out of her teens, and was pregnant. She was a long way from her homeland and her family, spoke very little English, and had not planned the pregnancy. She was not emotionally ready to be a mother and was struggling to cope with the idea. She had had a number of hospital appointments already, and some of the staff team had spent many hours supporting her emotionally and practically. There was one other complicating factor – she was having *triplets*. One of the babies had already died in the womb, and the doctors feared she might lose the other two. The appointment that day was to talk through her options, and the medical recommendation was that the birth should be induced as soon as possible to give the surviving twins the best possible chance of survival.

When this was suggested to her, she was adamant that she did not want to be induced. She wanted to go full term and trust God; whether that was faith or denial, I am not sure – perhaps a bit of both – but nothing would change her mind. At that point the doctor said that she would have to sign a document absolving the hospital of any culpability, should anything go wrong. Then came the question that was to change my thinking on how we did things at Boaz. 'Who is your next of kin?' she was asked.

'I have no family,' she replied. 'Boaz is my family.'

'Boaz is my family.' The words swirled around in my head and kept coming back to me throughout the day. 'Well,' I thought, 'if that is how she sees us, then maybe that's just what we ought to be – a family for all our clients.' Of course, not all Boaz residents need a great deal of support. Some are amazingly self-sufficient and need minimal support, little more than a roof over their heads. For others, Boaz is perhaps the only real support they have.

A few months later we had our first Family Night. We invited current and former Boaz residents, staff, trustees, supporters, volunteers – anyone who had been or still was 'Boaz family' – to come to a 'bring-and-share' meal. Now we have a Family Night every two or three months. Sometimes we sing; sometimes we have a short Bible message; sometimes someone shares some good news or we give out awards. There is always enough to eat. Some former clients bring delicious ethnic dishes. Others will get stuck in with setting up the chairs or the washing up. Everywhere people are chatting, meeting old friends or getting to know new ones. I love it.

At the end of one Family Night our oldest volunteer, who at the age of 80 was still driving people to the night shelter, said to me with a big smile on her face, 'This is what church should be like.' I didn't argue with her. Housing, advocacy, legal advice, classes, trips out: all of these are important, but nothing trumps the need for family.

Chapter 34
'If you want to walk on water, you've got to get out of the boat'

I started with this, and I'm going to finish with it. John Ortberg's book of the same name as this chapter should be compulsory reading for all Christians. No, he hasn't paid me to say that (though a few quid wouldn't go amiss). You see, it's not that Christians lack knowledge. At least, they have no excuse for lacking knowledge, as there are enough versions of the Bible, study guides and commentaries to fill every hour of every day. Knowledge is important. Action without knowledge is stupid. But the reverse is also true. However much knowledge we have, it's worthless if we do nothing with it.

Matthew tells the story in chapter 14 of his gospel of how Jesus walked across a lake during a storm at night. His disciples were struggling to row across the lake. Jesus came alongside the boat. At first they thought He was a ghost, but Peter shouted out, 'Lord, if it's really you, tell me to come to you, walking on the water' (Matthew 14:28). Jesus told him to come, and Peter climbed over the side and began to walk on the water. Halfway, he began to realise what he was doing: he saw the wind and waves, was scared, and started to sink, but Jesus reached out and pulled him up.

John Ortberg draws some fabulous lessons from this short story, lessons that apply to all of us. These are the things that struck me, and which I would like to leave with you:

1. Of the 12, only Peter walked on the water, because he was the only one who took a risk. The others were wet and cold anyway, but he experienced the walk of a lifetime!

2. Sure, he sank, but better to sink and be rescued by Jesus than never to sink because you haven't moved. God doesn't mind failures, but He doesn't like non-triers.

3. It all started with one step of faith, but it didn't end there. Peter, despite his failings, was the one to whom Jesus entrusted His Church.[117] That has to give us all hope!

So what is God calling you to do? I guarantee it won't be easy. It will cost. There will be times when you wonder what on earth you are doing, and probably what in heaven God is doing. But it will be worth it.

I have no idea what the future holds for me or for Boaz, though I do have some dreams that I think may be from God. They include growth and expansion of the Boaz family, breakthroughs in humane asylum legislation, churches full of asylum seekers and refugees who know Jesus, are fully integrated and are making an amazing contribution to society, a coalition with a voice so strong that it cannot be ignored by politicians, and a country that finally understands what it is like to be a refugee from your homeland.

I don't know whether I will be here to see them come to fruition, but I believe they will come to pass, because this isn't my work. It's God's, and He hasn't finished yet.

---

[117] Matthew 16:17-19; John 21:15-18.